*Shakespeare
and the Ideal of Love*

*Memorial busts of
(above)* William
Shakespeare, 1564–1616,
Holy Trinity Church,
Stratford-upon-Avon, and
(below) *Marsilio Ficino,
1433–1499, Cathedral of Florence*

Shakespeare and the Ideal of Love

JILL LINE

Inner Traditions
Rochester, Vermont

Inner Traditions
One Park Street
Rochester, Vermont 05767
www.InnerTraditions.com

LIBRARY OF CONGRESS CATALOGING-IN-PUBLICATION DATA

Line, Jill.
  [Shakespeare and the fire of love]
  Shakespeare and the ideal of love / Jill Line.
      p. cm.
  "Originally published in the United Kingdom in 2004 by Shepheard-Walwyn
(Publishers) Ltd. under the title: Shakespeare and the fire of love"—T.p. verso.
  Includes bibliographical references (p.   ) and index.
  ISBN-13: 978-1-59477-145-3 (pbk.)
  ISBN-10: 1-59477-145-6 (pbk.)
  1. Shakespeare, William, 1564–1616—Criticism and interpretation. 2. Love in
literature. 3. Ficino, Marsilio, 1433–1499. 4. Neoplatonism in literature. I. Title.
  PR3069.L6L56 2007
  822.3'3—dc22

                                                                2006022679

Printed and bound in the United States by Lake Book Manufacturing

10   9   8   7   6   5   4   3   2   1

This book was typeset in Aldine

Contents

List of Illustrations

To John

Acknowledgements

I SHOULD LIKE TO thank the following for their help, advice and inspiration: Kathleen Raine, Joseph Milne and students of the Temenos Academy, Sheila Rosenberg, Clement Salaman and members of the Renaissance Group of the School of Economic Science, Peter Dawkins, Mark Rylance, Tim Addey—and many other friends who have given their support.

In addition, I would like to thank Sears Jayne for permission to quote from his *Commentary on Plato's Symposium on Love*, Shepheard-Walwyn (Publishers) Ltd. for permission to quote from their edition of *The Letters of Marsilio Ficino* and the Prometheus Trust for permission to reproduce Diotima's Speech to Socrates from their edition of Plato's *Symposium*. I am grateful to the National Gallery in London for permission to reproduce Botticelli's *Venus and Mars* and Leonardo da Vinci's *Virgin of the Rocks*, and to Abbott Hall Art Gallery in Kendal for permission to use George Romney's *King Lear in the Tempest* on the cover.

For the quotations from Shakespeare I have used the Arden edition published by Methuen, London.

Preface

THIS BOOK is the culmination of my research over the last few years
for many lectures and essays on Shakespeare and Christian-Platonism.
These include a series of essays in booklet form written for the Globe
Theatre's season of Roman plays, a contribution to a book on Marsilio
Ficino[1] and lectures for the Temenos Academy and for the Prince of
Wales' Shakespeare School for Teachers with the Royal Shakespeare
Company.

My interest in this subject began in the 1970s when I first read John
Vyvyan's books on Shakespeare and the work of Dame Frances Yates on
Renaissance philosophy. At the same time I was introduced to Platonic
and Hermetic philosophy and, in particular, to the Christian-Platonic
writings and letters of the fifteenth century Florentine, Marsilio
Ficino. My own research began with a study of the Platonic concept
of love in the masques of Ben Jonson and Inigo Jones. It was not until
some years later, during a year spent at the Shakespeare Institute in
Stratford-upon-Avon, that I realised just how intrinsic these concepts
are to Shakespeare. Strangely, whilst Christian-Platonism has long
been associated with the poetry of many of his contemporaries, its
relationship to Shakespeare and his plays is not so well known. Jonson
had openly acknowledged his debt to the 'Platonicks' but I now found
that, with this philosophy in mind, the whole inner meaning of
Shakespeare's plays and poems began to fall into place.

It has not been possible to cover all the plays and poems in this
book and some are explored in greater depth than others. Most of
the comedies and some of the sonnets are mentioned as they show
most clearly the concepts of Christian-Platonic love, while the great
tragedies, some of the Roman plays and Shakespeare's last plays will
be used to show how he expanded on these ideas throughout his writing life. There is little reference to the histories since, although they

contain the ideals of Christian-Platonism, they follow a different path
and would be the subject of another book.

It has been an exciting journey and there is still far to go. Dis-
coveries are endless and, for this reason, it has been a difficult book
to complete. Many would agree that, each time Shakespeare's words
are heard afresh, something new is realised. This is true, of course, on
whatever level Shakespeare's plays are taken, whether for their plots or
their politics; but, if the greater riches they contain are to be unlocked,
there needs to be some sort of ground-plan, an understanding of his
underlying philosophy. The aim of this book, therefore, is to provide
that ground-plan so that readers may be inspired to discover more for
themselves and with 'I see!' to experience a flash of Shakespeare's own
inspiration.

CHAPTER ONE

Ficino and the Platonic Worlds

From women's eyes this doctrine I derive: They
are the ground, the books, the academes, From
whence doth spring the true Promethean fire
4.3.298–300

T HESE WORDS, spoken by Berowne in *Love's Labours Lost,*
embody all the passions of the early stages of love. What
young man would desire to bury himself in his studies when
a woman's flashing eyes tempt him to a learning experience of a quite
different nature. But Berowne seems to be saying far more than this.
Within a woman's eyes, often called the windows or mirrors of the
soul, the whole world may be revealed, encompassed and given nour-
ishment. It is not so much the eyes themselves as the light or fire, the
true Promethean fire, with which they sparkle, that carries this true
knowledge to the lover. What does Shakespeare really mean by this and
what is the true Promethean fire? The answers lie in the Christian-
Platonic philosophy of love in which all Shakespeare's plays and
poems have their genesis. In its most immediate form, it may be traced
to the Florentine philosopher Marsilio Ficino who had lived a century
earlier.

With the intention to 'demystify', most Shakespearean criticism of
recent years has been set firmly in the historical, social and political
context of our contemporary world. Whilst an academic deconstruc-
tion of his language may unearth a multiplicity of approaches, there
is no need to tear Shakespeare apart in order to find a meaning for
audiences today. The meaning is there, in his words, his themes and
his poetry, a meaning that goes beyond current political issues, beyond
gender and race, to the ideas, forms and universal laws that lie beyond
the material world and have their roots in one source. It is from this

point that Shakespeare viewed creation and from which he was able to write of such universal themes as the harmony and disharmony between nations and princes and the inner conflicts of mind and soul in men and women whose natures and desires are not confined to any particular age.

The philosophy by which he was guided is perennial and has passed from the mists of time through a long line of teachers including Hermes Tristmegistus, Pythagoras, Plato and Plotinus. The one philosopher of this tradition, however, whose ideas Shakespeare most clearly reflects was a scholar-priest living in fifteenth-century Florence named Marsilio Ficino. It was he who drew the strands of many teachings together and, having found the same truths in Christianity, formulated a philosophy that is generally referred to today as Christian-Platonism.

The son of Cosimo de' Medici's physician, Marsilio Ficino was born in Florence in 1433 and became a philosopher, priest, doctor, astrologer and a highly accomplished musician, skilled on the lyre. Under the patronage of the de' Medici family, he was the founder and leader of the Platonic Academy in Florence, where he himself was responsible for the translations, from Greek into Latin, of Plato, Hermes Tristmegistus, the Orphic hymns and neo-Platonists such as Plotinus and Porphyry. Many of the manuscripts he used had been recovered by Cosimo's agents from remote monasteries where they had lain, lost to the world, for centuries. The academy, whose members included Lorenzo de' Medici and the philosopher-poet Pico della Mirandola, inspired a renaissance of the arts in Florence that spread over the whole of Italy and across Europe.

Among Ficino's correspondents, who included some of the most influential men in Europe, was John Colet, Dean of St Paul's Cathedral and the founder of St Paul's School. It was he who helped to promote Ficino's teachings in England and it was not long before translations and commentaries by Ficino were to be found in the university libraries. Ficino's philosophy, known at the time as the new learning, became well known in academic and artistic circles and was soon inspiring the poets and artists of the English Renaissance. In 1578, when Shakespeare was fourteen, a work that was to provide a framework for his inspiration, Ficino's *De Amore,* a commentary on Plato's *Symposium on Love*, became more widely known when it was translated into French.

Ficino always referred to his commentary as *De Amore* or the Book of Love. Sears Jayne's excellent translation is titled *Commentary on Plato's Symposium on Love* and therefore will be referred to in the notes at the end of this book as the *Commentary*, but wherever it is mentioned in the following pages it will be given Ficino's Italian title.

Although Castiglione's *Book of the Courtier*, translated into English in 1561, has been more widely recognised as a source of the new learning, it still owes its philosophy of love to Ficino and *De Amore*. Spenser, Chapman and Donne were among the many poets inspired by this philosophy of love, as it was also called, and the court masques of Ben Jonson and Inigo Jones were steeped in Platonic imagery. So whether or not Shakespeare read *De Amore* himself, he was growing up in a society imbued with Ficino's form of Christian-Platonism.

In one of his many letters to his friends and pupils, Ficino wrote that 'it was the chief work of the divine Plato. . . to reveal the principle of unity in all things',[1] a phrase that encapsulates not only the chief work of Ficino himself but also that of Shakespeare for, as his plays and poems reveal, the principle of unity was their foundation. Adding the dimension of Christianity to the Platonic teaching, Ficino tended to refer to this principle of unity as God, although he also used the Platonic terms of the One or the Good.

The One is the source of all creation and its many worlds. From the One comes multiplicity and form; as each world expands into the next its forms increase and become more dense. The full Platonic model contains six worlds but Ficino simplifies them into three, or sometimes four.[2] The first world is that of Mind: although often translated as Intellect, it is far above ordinary thought and reason. Since it is the world of the angels and the gods, Ficino calls it the Angelic Mind and, as we shall discover in a later chapter, it is also the world of creative imagination. Next comes the realm of the Soul and finally the Body of the World, the whole of the material world that we perceive through our senses. The body is ornamented by Nature, which Ficino refers to sometimes as a separate, fourth world. All that lies in the upper part of the soul and the angelic mind pertains to the heavens, whilst the lower part of the soul and all beneath belongs to the earthly world.

As Ficino tells it in *De Amore*, creation is a love story for, as each world is created, it falls in love with the beauty of the higher world

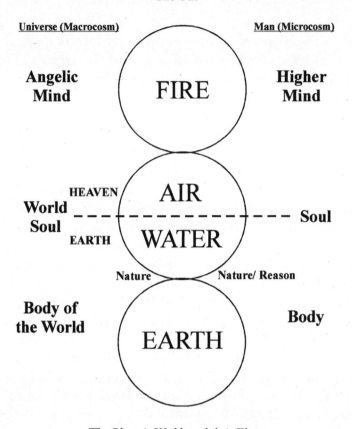

The Platonic Worlds and their Elements

and, from that love, a new world is created. As there are three worlds so there are three chaoses, by which Ficino means dark unformed nothingness. The chaos of the unformed angelic mind lies in the mind of God, the creator. This initial essence of mind falls in love with its creator and thus becomes the first act of love. From their union, the angelic world is given form. In the creation of the other worlds, love remains the activating force. The unformed chaos of the soul, falling in love with the angelic mind, gives birth to the world of the soul. Likewise the material world is born:

> In the same way, the Matter of this world, although in the beginning it lay a formless chaos, without the ornament of Forms, immediately because of a love innate in itself, it directed itself toward the Soul and offered itself obedient to it, and through this conciliating love,

receiving from the Soul the ornament of all the Forms which are seen in this world, from a Chaos became a world.[3]

This act did not occur once, at the beginning of time, but is an on-going process and, as the worlds manifest on the universal scale, so they are also to be found within each individual being. Man[4] is a universe in the microcosm and, like the macrocosm, is composed of the same worlds of mind, soul, nature and body. For both the universe and for every human being, each moment has its own creative potential.

Now the innate beauty of each world, whether in the macrocosm of the universe or the microcosm of a human being, is illuminated by a ray that lights the beauty of each world and, through its light, inspires love for that beauty. Ficino calls it 'the one truth, which is the single ray of the one God'.[5]

The divine ray, lighting beauty and inspiring love, acts as the creative power of God in forming the universe. It also acts as a guide, to those who so desire it, to return to the source of their being and become unified in God. Passing through all higher worlds on our journey into creation, we find ourselves in a corporeal body, living in the material world and ornamented with our nature. But we are all given the opportunity to discover those higher worlds of which, imprisoned as we are in our bodies, we may have only an occasional glimpse. The return journey is also through love, being the act of creation in reverse. Those who search are first attracted by the outward beauty of the physical world, then the lover progresses through love of the beauty of virtue, the beauty of soul and the beauty of mind. Finally the soul is seized by the brilliance of divine beauty itself and, drawn upward as if by a hook, itself becomes God. Ficino writes of this in a letter to his close friend, Giovanni Cavalcanti, who first urged him to write De Amore:

> . . . the single ray of the one God. . . shines in every individual thing according to its nature and is called grace and beauty; and where it shines more clearly, it especially attracts the man who is watching, stimulates him who thinks, and catches and possesses him who draws near to it. This ray also compels him to revere its splendour more than all else, as if it were a divine spirit, and, once his former nature has been cast aside, to strive for nothing else but to become this splendour. . . The soul, consumed by the divine brilliance which shines in the beauteous man as though in a mirror, is seized

unknowingly by that brilliance, and is drawn upward as by a hook, so that the soul becomes God.[6]

In this way the divine ray, that lights beauty and inspires love, becomes the path to unity with God. It is the path on which Shakespeare's lovers embark and it is the goal to which they aspire. In truth, all Shakespeare's heroes are lovers for, as Ficino points out, the two words have the same derivation: 'All are called heroes, that is, lovers, from the Greek word "heros" which means "love".'[7] As we shall discover in some plays, such as *Love's Labours Lost,* the lovers have hardly started upon their journey, while Bassanio in *The Merchant of Venice,* is well on his way before the play opens.

Before we begin to explore these plays, it would be helpful to look at the court masques that were being performed in Shakespeare's lifetime. These masques are overtly Platonic and shed much light on what is not, at first, quite so obvious in Shakespeare's plays. Written for performance at the court of King James I by Ben Jonson and others, they are allegories of the ascent of love and depict the Platonic worlds through their poetry, songs and dance, and the stage designs of Inigo Jones. When the first masque of Jonson and Jones' long and often stormy partnership was performed in 1605, James had just ascended the throne and taken over the patronage of Shakespeare's company. In consequence the King's Men, as they were now known, increased their number of court appearances, many of which took place during the winter season alongside the preparations for the annual masque. It is fair to suppose that the King's Men and the masque-makers took a mutual interest in each other's productions and that their two writers discussed their work, finding common interest in 'the Platonicks' opinion', as Jonson annotated his *Masque of Beauty.* The many notes that Jonson made so helpfully on his manuscripts make one wonder what marginalia Shakespeare might have written!

The masques were costly extravaganzas, usually performed once a year as part of the Christmas festivities, although occasionally one was specially commissioned for a particular celebration such as an important wedding. There was much competition among the court ladies to take part and, often including Queen Anne herself, they would appear as heavenly beauties of the soul. They bedecked themselves in dazzling costumes and did little but pose and dance gracefully, endeavouring to attract the love of the gentlemen courtiers, and the audience, with their beauty. The gentlemen played the lovers' roles as they set out on the path of love: the intention was to take the audience with them on their journey and, in the formal style of the masque that was very like a ritual, to give them a glimpse of the higher worlds.

Man enters a golden age and moves with perfect ease from earth to heaven; and most to the point, this vision, at its climactic moment includes us, the mortal spectator; we, too, are transformed by the power of knowledge and reason.[8]

The final union was expressed through a dance in which the masquers joined the audience in the dancing space before the throne:

Every masque moved towards the moment when the masquers descended and took partners from the audience, annihilating the barrier between the ideal and the real and including the court in its miraculous transformation.[9]

Inigo Jones' elaborate designs for the sets and costumes, many of them extant, are also rich in the imagery of love and the Christian-Platonic worlds. Fortunately, Jonson described them very carefully in the published editions of his work; although the design itself has been lost, his description of the set for *Hymenaei*, a wedding masque performed in 1606, is particularly helpful in its representation of the Platonic worlds.

The elaborate and very expensive setting is on three levels, the highest reaching to the roof of the Whitehall Palace banqueting hall, where the masque was performed. On the lowest level stands a huge globe painted with countries and seas which, when it is revolved, reveals a jewel-encrusted mine sparkling in the candlelight; this symbolises earth, the physical world. Arranged in elegant attitudes inside are eight gentlemen of the court dressed as the four humours of melancholy, phlegm, blood and choler and the four affections of desire, joy, fear and grief; in other words they represent the various natures and emotions of mankind belonging to the material world. Seated on top of the globe, controlling these earthly passions but still part of the same world, is Reason, a female figure dressed in a long blue robe, sequinned with stars and arithmetical figures. As the illuminator of

Inigo Jones' design for Love Freed from Ignorance and Folly, *1612.*

the mind, she holds up a lamp, and with raised sword she points the way to higher worlds.

On the second level, representing the world of the soul, eight court ladies display their elegant silver and white costumes. The illustration of Jones' set for a later masque, *Love Freed from Ignorance and Folly*, gives some idea of how this middle world may have appeared. Each world has a particular element, those belonging to the body and the lower part of the soul being earth and water, while air symbolises the heavenly part of the soul and fire the angelic mind. For this reason the ladies are seated against a background of dark rain-clouds, representing the soul's elements of air and water. Beside the ladies stands Iris, goddess of the rainbow that bridges heaven and earth and is also composed of air and water. The soul is where these realms may meet in harmony, so Iris is accompanied by musicians who provide the heavenly harmony that the poets called the music of the spheres. Above them all stands the goddess Juno, queen of the soul.

Above Juno is set the heavenly world of the angelic mind. This region of fire is ruled by Jupiter: Inigo Jones portrays him in classical style as a huge figure brandishing a thunderbolt above a fiery area, ingeniously contrived by a multitude of whirling coloured lanterns.

The completion of the set lay in the audience, in the person of the King. By the divine right of kings, the monarch represented God on earth and, during the court entertainments, his throne was placed in the centre of the banqueting hall, at the point where all sight lines from the stage met. These represented the rays of creation, radiating out into the universe from the Godhead, the source of all the worlds.

In his introduction to *Hymenaei*, Jonson wrote that the masques were intended not only to dazzle the eyes with their 'outward show', but also to 'furnish the inward parts'. Shakespeare frequently warns against taking the outward show of the material world at its face value for, as Bassanio wisely remarks when trying to make the right choice from the three caskets:

> So may the outward shows be least themselves,
> The world is still deceived with ornament.
> *Merchant of Venice* 3.2.73–4

The following exploration of love and the Platonic worlds in Shakespeare's work is undertaken with the intention of looking beyond the ornament of the outward show and, by furnishing the inward parts, of discovering how Shakespeare, following in the footsteps of Ficino and Plato, also revealed 'the principle of unity in all things'.

CHAPTER TWO

Cupid's Dart

———•·•———

O NCE BORN into the physical world, human beings quickly forget the unity from which they have sprung and see only multiplicity. But as there is an outward movement of creation that stems from the One, so there is a return for, if man so desires, he may be drawn back to his source through the power of love. This is achieved by following a clearly defined route on which the priestess, Diotima, instructs Socrates in *The Symposium*.[1] In Ficino's words, it is a path that 'by restoring us, formerly divided, to a whole, leads us back to heaven'.[2]

Love is awoken by beauty. The beauty of every world is a reflection of the beauty of God and, by falling in love with the beauty of each world, it is possible to rediscover its source. Thus the first step in the return to this divine beauty is to fall in love with the beauty of an outward form in the material world. This may be a work of nature or of art but, to Renaissance poets like Shakespeare, it is invariably the beauty of a woman that attracts the lover first setting out on this path. Shakespeare, like other Renaissance poets, follows the convention that, when women first attract love through their beauty, they become personifications of men's souls. 'Women,' wrote Ben Jonson, 'are the souls of men.'[3]

The lovers in *Love's Labours Lost* are on their first steps along the path of love. During the course of the play they find their true soulmates and discover that love is more than desire for an outward form and physical gratification. Falling in love with the outward beauty of the Princess and her ladies, the lovers woo with fanciful verses and make fools of themselves in the guise of Russians. By the end of the play they have progressed in the love game so far as to declare their love honestly and openly.

Before the Princess of France and her attendants arrive at the Court of Navarre, the King had resolved to withdraw from the world for three years to lead a monastic life without women and to spend his time studying philosophy with his companions. This little academy will, he believes, bring fame to himself and his court. Their resolve is short lived for they have not yet set foot on the first step of the spiritual path, which entails falling in love. And so, unwilling to appear rude when the ladies unexpectedly arrive, they entertain them and the game of love begins.

Their mistresses not only represent the heavenly beauty of their souls with which they may, when they have proved themselves, be joined in the union of marriage but, as is customary in all these comedies of love, they also act as the men's tutors. So they are set on the next step by the ladies' giving them tasks to perform that will enable them to love the good, the virtues of the higher world and the true beauty of their beloved. In this way they are given the opportunity to discover the virtues lying hidden within their own souls, which will make them worthy of marriage. The Princess tells the King to follow the austere life he had earlier proposed, this time not for the fame he had first desired, but to discover the true virtues of goodness, constancy and patience:

> If this austere insociable life
> Change not your offer made in heat of blood;
> If frosts and fasts, hard lodging and thin weeds,
> Nip not the gaudy blossoms of your love,
> But that it bear this trial and last love;
> Then at the expiration of the year,
> Come challenge me, challenge me by these deserts,
> And, by this virgin palm now kissing thine,
> I will be thine.

> 5.2.791–9

On the other hand, Rosaline sends Berowne to a hospital where his customary mocking wit and biting tongue may be turned to kindly use, to help rather than hurt:

> You shall this twelve month term from day to day,
> Visit the speechless sick, and still converse

With groaning wretches; and your task shall be
With all the fierce endeavour of your wit
To enforce the pained impotent to smile.

5.2.842–6

Throughout the play Berowne has had more insight into the Platonic
ascent of love than the other young men. Punning on the word 'light'
by referring to eyes as light, he scorns study as a way to darkness rather
than light since, he says, reading wears out the eyes and will lead to the
darkness of the blind rather than to enlightenment! The only true light,
he insists, lies dazzling in a woman's eyes:

Light seeking light doth light of light beguile:
So, ere you find where light in darkness lies,
Your light grows dark by losing of your eyes.
Study me how to please the eye indeed,
By fixing it upon a fairer eye,
Who dazzling so, that eye shall be his heed,
And give him light that he was blinded by.

1.1.77–83

When they have all finally admitted their love to each other, Berowne
reassures them that they have followed the right course and that they
will indeed learn more from a lady's eyes than through any book:

From women's eyes this doctrine I derive:
They sparkle still the right Promethean fire;
They are the books, the arts, the academes,
That show, contain, and nourish all the world;

4.3.346–9

This variation on the quotation at the beginning of the first chapter is
due to repetition, probably resulting from the early mingling of two
manuscripts.[4]

The true lover, although first attracted by the beauty of form, will
come to realise that it is the splendour of divine light sparkling in the
eyes of the beloved that mirrors the soul to itself and draws the lover
forward on his path. Berowne calls this light the true, or right, Promethean fire, referring to the original fire that Prometheus stole from
the gods for the benefit of mankind. This gift was far greater than the

THE
TEMPEST.

ordinary light and warmth of physical fire. It is the essential fire, the splendour of God, whose ray lights the beauty of all worlds and that lovers see sparkling in the eyes of their beloved. Although in this passage he is using the masculine gender, Ficino is describing how the sight of this fire in the eyes of either sex both awakens and attracts the soul:

> A man's appearance, which is often very beautiful to see, on account of an interior goodness fortunately given him by God, can send a ray of its splendour through the eyes of those who see him and into their soul. Drawn by this spark as if by a kind of hook, the soul hastens towards the drawer.[5]

This Promethean fire, illuminating the beauty of all the worlds in a shaft of light, has another symbol in the arrow of love shot by Cupid's bow. So often depicted piercing red hearts on Valentine cards and carved by generations of lovers into trees and stones, its true significance lies in the divine ray. At the first sight of the beauty of his beloved, the heart of the lover is pierced by Cupid's dart. 'Shot, by heaven', says Berowne with great delight as he overhears the King composing his first love-letter, 'Proceed, sweet Cupid. Thou hast thumped him with thy bird-bolt under the left pap!' (4.3.21–2). The same image, generally delivered in a more elevated style, occurs throughout the comedies and poems, always alerting us to the lover's awakening to heavenly beauty.

Ficino, following Plato, writes of two Cupids, the first being the divine love that flows out through the worlds, both creating the worlds and drawing them home, like the exhalation and inhalation of breath. The other love flies between the heavenly and earthly worlds on the wings of the familiar cherubic Cupid; he shoots the ray of divine light into the heart of the lover, but there is always the chance that he may lead him in the wrong direction. The original love, arising at the first moment of creation, is said to have no parents and is called the oldest of the gods, while the younger Cupid was born of Venus. The two forms of love are depicted as old and young Cupids on several headpieces in the First Folio, including Shakespeare's dedication to the Earls of Pembroke and Montgomery, the list of all the plays in the volume and *The Tempest*, the first play in the Folio. This first complete edition of Shakespeare's plays, published in 1623, seven years after Shakespeare's death, was assembled by his close friends and it is clear that they had full understanding of the works they were presenting to the world. The inclusion of the Cupid headpiece[6] on the dedication, the catalogue of plays and the opening play indicates the important part love plays in the canon. Yet another Cupid headpiece occurs above the Epilogue for *Henry IV Part 2*. The speech, probably added for a court performance, is addressed to Queen Elizabeth, regarded as the earthly representation of divine love.

By the opening of *The Merchant of Venice*, Bassanio has already come to appreciate the virtue as well as the beauty of the woman he desires to marry; her eyes, he tells his friend, Antonio, convey the light of love:

> In Belmont is a lady richly left,
> And she is fair, and (fairer than that word),
> Of wondrous virtues,—sometimes from her eyes
> I did receive fair speechless messages:
> Her name is Portia, . . .

> 1.1.161–4

Bassanio has reached the point on the path of love when he must be guided to the world of the soul by reason. On Inigo Jones' staging for *Hymeniae*, Reason sits above the material world and its conflicting nature, both controlling it and pointing with her sword towards higher worlds. Thus, faced with the daunting task of choosing one of the three caskets that will win him Portia's hand in marriage and lead him into the world of the soul, it is reason that comes to Bassanio's aid. As he

makes his choice, the words of a song being played by the musicians
urge the death of fancy, 'Let us all ring Fancy's knell' (3.2.70). This is a
subtle hint from Portia, now acting as his tutor in love, not to be ruled
by his desires and emotions as the previous suitors were, but to keep a
clear head. Bassanio then gives a reasoned discourse on the dangers of
being deceived by outward appearances:

> So may the outward shows be least themselves,—
> The world is still deceiv'd by ornament—
> In law, what plea so tainted and corrupt,
> But being season'd with a gracious voice,
> Obscures the show of evil?
> . . .
> Thus ornament is but the guiled shore
> To a most dangerous sea: the beauteous scarf
> Veiling an Indian beauty; in a word,
> The seeming truth which cunning times put on
> To entrap the wisest.
>
> 3.2.73–101

By enabling him to look beyond the superficial values of this world
and discard the gold and silver for the least attractive lead, his love of
virtuous beauty, aided by reason, points to the right choice of casket:

> Therefore thou gaudy gold,
> Hard food for Midas, I will none of thee,
> Nor none of thee thou pale and common drudge
> 'Tween man and man: but thou, thou meagre lead
> Which rather threaten'st than thou dost promise aught,
> Thy paleness moves me more than eloquence,
> And here choose I.
>
> 3.2.101–7

This speech may be compared with Ficino's warning against deceptive
appearances in his description of the true gold of the soul lying hidden
within an unpromising shell:

> When the earthly grime has been removed you will at once see pure
> gold, and when the clouds have been dispersed, you will see the
> clear sky.[7]

So Bassanio finds in the leaden casket the portrait of Portia—the true gold.

A danger for the intending lover of heavenly beauty is that he will be mistaken in his love for, as there are two Cupids, so there are two Venuses. It is the beauty of the higher that, filled with the true Promethean fire, draws the true lover towards God. The other, earthly Venus may lead in either direction for, although her finer purpose is to reproduce the beauty of God through procreation, she has also the propensity to fall into mere lust:

> The soul again possesses twin powers. It certainly has the power of understanding, and it has the power of procreation. These twin powers are two Venuses in us, accompanied by twin loves. When the beauty of a human body first meets our eyes, our intellect, which is the first Venus in us, worships and esteems it as an image of the divine beauty, and through this is often aroused to that. But the power of procreation, the second Venus, desires to procreate a form like this. On both sides, therefore, there is a love: there a desire to contemplate beauty, here a desire to propagate it. Each love is virtuous and praiseworthy, for each follows a divine image.[8]

In *Romeo and Juliet*, Romeo is mistaken in his first love for Rosaline, over whom he has fallen into a black depression. Drawn by her outward appearance, he believes her to be his soul-mate but, instead of lightness of heart, he finds nothing but reversal, chaos and disharmony:

> O brawling love, O loving hate,
> O anything, of nothing first create!
> O heavy lightness, serious vanity,
> Misshapen chaos of well-seeming forms,
> Feather of lead, bright smoke, cold fire, sick health,
> Still-waking sleep, that is not what it is!
>
> 1.1.174–9

Heavy with misery, he is unwilling to dance with his friends. 'You are a lover,' Mercutio tells him, 'borrow Cupid's wings / And soar with them above a common bound,' but Romeo replies that he is 'too sore empierced with his shaft / To soar with his light feathers. . . Under love's heavy burden do I sink' (1.4.17–22). Romeo's problem is that his love is misplaced: eager to enter on the path of love, he has chosen a woman on whom, as Friar Lawrence has told him, he dotes rather than loves. The world of appearances can delude and, in this situation, Cupid's dart and wings encumber rather than aid love. Right judgement is vital for the lover: as soon as his eyes alight on Juliet he realises how mistaken his love has been and that he 'ne'er saw true beauty till this night' (1.5.52). Now, truly pierced by the ray of beauty, he recognises that the beauty of Juliet stems from the splendour of God himself for, as it is said in *De Amore*,

> true love is nothing other than a certain effort of flying up to divine beauty, aroused by the sight of corporeal beauty.[9]

Thus, using the form of a sonnet, Shakespeare turns the first meeting of Romeo and Juliet into a religious ritual: he presents Romeo as a pilgrim approaching a shrine; the kiss requested from Juliet is received as a blessing. Now, no longer weighed down with the heaviness of a misplaced love, Romeo soars with 'love's light wings' over the orchard wall to where Juliet stands on her balcony. In a letter explaining Plato's description of the soul in *Phaedrus*, Ficino writes how mortal beings

> do not fly back to heaven, whence they fell by weight of their earthly thoughts, until they begin to contemplate once more those divine natures which they have forgotten.[10]

Romeo is now at the point where, having seen the reflection of divine beauty in his beloved, the lover will remember that, before he became imprisoned in the body, he knew that beauty face to face. Fired by this memory, the soul will shake its wings and 'strives with all its might to reach the heavens'.[11] The first impression that Romeo has of Juliet is of the light she radiates, 'O, she doth teach the torches to burn bright!' (1.5.43), and it is this light that will lead him to truth:

> The beauty of bodies is a light; the beauty of the soul is also a light. The light of the soul is truth.[12]

When next he sees her on the balcony, he addresses her as the sun, the physical representation of the light of God:

for just as the sun gives warmth and light to the body, so God offers the light of truth and the warmth of love to souls.[13]

Before he leaves her garden he knows her as his soul: 'It is my soul that calls upon my name' (2.2.164), the heavenly part of his soul that is calling him. In the consummation of their marriage, the whole soul comes together as one. In a comedy this would be the end of the play, but the lovers also represent two sides of a divided society whose harmony has been disrupted. Separated by strife, it is not until their final reunion in death that peace may be restored.

Orsino, the love-sick duke in *Twelfth Night*, is another lover who mistakes his soul-mate but, unlike Romeo, it is not until the end of the play that he recognises the true recipient of his love. He is impatient to begin hunting the 'hart', a metaphor favoured by Shakespeare for the initial stages of love, but, caught in a world of fancy and desire, his love is misplaced. His depression and mixed emotions over Olivia are very like Romeo's for Rosaline and there are the same dark images. Instead of the Promethean fire of true love that distinguishes Juliet from her predecessor, Orsino remembers not the light that Olivia brought but the darkness that she dispelled:

> O, when mine eyes did see Olivia first,
> Methought she purged the air of pestilence.
> That instant was I turned into a hart,
> And my desires, like fell and cruel hounds,
> E'er since pursue me.
>
> 1.1.19–23

The hunter of heavenly love has become the hunted driven to earth.

Yet Orsino, again like Romeo, understands the meaning of love, although his knowledge is, as yet, theoretical. Olivia is too preoccupied with mourning the death of her brother to have any time for suitors until, of course, she finds her own soul-mate. Believing herself to be in love with Viola disguised as Cesario, she also misses the mark, until Sebastian appears. For her they are the twin Cupids; caught by appearances, her love for Viola is the earthly form that leads her to the heavenly love of Sebastian.

Orsino reflects how such sisterly love as Olivia has for her dead brother might flower into something much greater, not just for the happy recipient, but also into a love that encompasses the whole ideal of Christian-Platonism:

> How will she love, when the rich golden shaft
> Hath killed the flock of all affections else
> That live in her; when liver, brain, and heart,
> These sovereign thrones, are all supplied and filled—
> Her sweet perfections—with one self king.
>
> 1.1.35–9

The rich golden shaft of Cupid's dart, the true Promethean fire, will bring the humours and affections of the physical body or world under control. Liver, brain and heart are related to the three worlds of body, mind and soul in the microcosm of man, thus, when they are 'all supplied and filled' and brought together in the completeness of love, your self, the 'one self king', will be known. As the inscription over the doorway to the Delphic oracle said, 'Know thyself.'

The true object of Orsino's love appears early in the play but, as the personification of unrecognised love, she is in disguise. Viola, shipwrecked on the shores of Illyria, assumes the appearance of a boy in order to survive in an alien land and finds employment as a page at Orsino's court. Whilst acting as a messenger between her master and his misplaced love, Olivia, she is unable to express the love she herself feels for him and can make only veiled hints:

> My father had a daughter loved a man—
> As it might be perhaps, were I a woman
> I should your lordship.
>
> 2.4.108–10

Viola, like the Princess of France and Portia, is Orsino's tutor in love and, through her restraint, self-sacrifice and constancy, she teaches him the nature of true love; thus, for much of the play, Orsino is serving his apprenticeship. When he begins to fall in love with her, it is not with her appearance, because she is disguised, but with the virtues of her soul. There are those who worry that, having lost Olivia to Sebastian in the last scene, Orsino's change of heart at the disclosure of Viola's true identity is too rapid. But it is to her soul, with which he has become familiar, that he is now able to declare his love, rather than to her outward form which he has yet to see in women's clothes. That he now has a proper understanding of love is shown by his prediction that, on their wedding day, it will be their souls that are joined in union:

> A solemn combination shall be made
> Of our dear souls.
>
> 5.1.382–3

From the start of *As You Like It*, Orlando is a step further along the path of love than the love-sick Orsino in the first scene of *Twelfth Night*. Orsino's love is misplaced but, when Orlando first sees Rosalind at her uncle's court, he chooses her correctly as the object of his love. In the manner of all true lovers he is first attracted by her outward beauty, addressing her as 'Fair Princess' (1.2.159) and, spurred on by her good wishes, wins a trial of physical strength in the wrestling match against the champion. Ending the scene with 'but heavenly Rosalind!' (1.3.279) proves he has begun to appreciate her heavenly beauty and is now prepared for the tests of the soul. Berowne and his comrades write poems to their mistresses at this stage and Orlando follows the same course with even greater vigour. Once in the forest, he decks the trees with poems praising both her beauty and her virtues:

> O Rosalind, these trees shall be my books,
> And in their barks my thoughts I'll character,
> That every eye which in this forest looks,
> Shall see thy virtue witness'd everywhere.
> Run, run Orlando, carve on every tree
> The fair, the chaste, and unexpressive she.
>
> 3.2.5–10

His first effort extols the beauty of her face:

> All the pictures fairest lin'd
> Are but black to Rosalind.
> Let no face be kept in mind
> But the fair of Rosalind.
>
> 3.2.90–3

But, in the next of his poetic offerings, he is writing of her graces and virtue:

L V C R E C E.

> Therefore Heaven Nature charg'd
> That one body should be fill'd
> With all graces wide-enlarg'd. . .
>
> 3.2.138–40

Although this signifies that Orlando now recognises her beauty of soul, he has still to learn it within himself and again he is taught by that higher part of his own soul. So Rosalind, having disguised her outward appearance in male attire, begins her task of teaching Orlando the true meaning of love.

Shakespeare uses cross-dressing in a number of plays. Ostensibly heroines dress as boys in order to make their way more easily in the harsh world into which they have been thrown, but in truth the disguise serves to veil their outward beauty so that lovers may learn to love the greater beauty within. Orsino loves physical beauty in the form of Olivia, who is not even his rightful love, until he learns to love the beauty of soul in his pageboy, the disguised Viola. Both Julia in *Two Gentlemen of Verona* and Imogen in *Cymbeline,* having been rejected by their lovers, dress as boys, not only to ease their passage as they journey in search of them, but also to teach them the true meaning of loving the soul. The revelation of the outward appearance of each when the veil of disguise is dropped is a sacred moment, for the lover sees not only the outer beauty that first drew him towards her but, for the first time, he sees the beauty of soul shining through in her true glory. This revelation is often depicted in the emblems of the Renaissance as the head of a bride whose veil has fallen. It appears on a number of headpieces in the Folio and other works, including the title-page of the first quarto edition, 1594, of his long poem, *Lucrece.*

The true significance may now be appreciated of Orlando's wooing of his love by proxy in the form of Ganymede, the disguised Rosalind. Ganymede was the name of the cupbearer to the gods, which places Rosalind firmly in the heavenly world. Rosalind mocks Orlando for not having the dishevelled and neglected appearance of a lover and offers, if he is really in love, to cure him of this love-sickness. This would entail treating her as if she were truly Rosalind and obeying all her whims. At first he is dubious and then spontaneously takes the next step towards loving the beauty of his soul by making a declaration of faith, 'Now by the faith of my love I will.' She next asks if he will go with her and he offers his heart, the symbol of the soul: 'With all my heart, good youth' (3.2.416– 21). Good humoured trials of love follow, in which Rosalind plays out the capriciousness of the humours and affections of the world to bring Orlando to a knowledge of his own virtues and to learn the constancy of love. But the true virtue of his soul is only seriously established when he rescues the brother who had formerly treated him so badly, even to the point of trying to take his life, from a lioness about to attack him as he lies sleeping under a tree. Although tempted to avenge himself by leaving his brother to the mercies of the lioness, compassion gets the better of him, as his brother Oliver himself later tells Rosalind and Celia:

> Twice did he turn his back, and purpos'd so.
> But kindness, nobler ever than revenge,
> And nature, stronger than his just occasion,
> Made him give battle to the lioness,
> Who quickly fell before him—
>
> 4.3.127–31

It is interesting that the wild beast he overcomes is a lion, a symbol not only of courage but also of the sun, which in turn represents the soul. It acts here as a guardian to the world of the soul which needs to be overcome by some act of virtue in order for the lover to enter that world. Orlando's generous nature overcomes any feeling of revenge for his brother and his act of mercy enables him to become united with his soul. His courage and true love not only win him the heart and hand of Rosalind, but his merciful deed has the effect of converting his brother, who becomes bitterly ashamed of his former behaviour. Indeed, Oliver's conversion is so strong that he is able to accompany Orlando into the world of the soul and win immediate union with his beloved whom, in the form of Celia, he has no hesitation in recognising. Each degree of love is accomplished within a timeless moment, for they:

> No sooner met, but they looked; no sooner looked, but they loved; no sooner loved, but they sighed; no sooner sighed, but they asked one another the reason; no sooner knew the reason, but they sought the remedy. And in these degrees have they made a pair of stairs to marriage.
>
> 5.2.31–7

As Orlando has recognised true love, the veil hiding love may be dropped and, casting off her disguise as a boy, Rosalind appears at their wedding dressed as a bride with her veil lowered and her face revealed. At this moment, before their union in marriage, Orlando can at last see heavenly beauty, the face of truth itself. Hymen, the god of marriage, himself conducts the ceremony which ends in song:

> Wedding is great Juno's crown,
> O blessed bond of board and bed.
> 'Tis Hymen peoples every town;
> High wedlock then be honoured.
>
> 5.4.140–3

Although the words appear to celebrate the physical union of marriage, the acknowledgement of Juno who, as in the masque of *Hymeniae*, represents the union of the soul, sets the wedding of Rosalind and Orlando in the same context.

Three other couples are married at the same time as Orlando and Rosalind: the speedily united Oliver and Celia, Silvius the shepherd and his beloved Phoebe, and the amorous, earthy pair, Touchstone and Audrey. 'Every one chooses his love from the ranks of beauty according to his own character,' wrote Plato,[14] and Touchstone, being a clown who reflects through his wit the character of whomsoever he comes into contact with and is therefore a many-sided character himself, chooses a down-to-earth love in the form of Audrey. Resigned to his fate, Touchstone proposes to Audrey in suitably earthy terms, 'Well, praised be the gods for thy foulness; sluttishness may come hereafter. But be that as it may be, I will marry thee' (3.3.34–6).

The name Phoebe is synonymous with the Roman Diana, Artemis in her Greek form, the chaste goddess of the moon who rules over the world of nature inhabited by this pair of lovers. Phoebe is loved by Silvius, a shepherd of the sylvan woodland. His wooing is at first in vain for, in an interesting twist, Phoebe, the heavenly beauty to whom he aspires, falls in love with Rosalind, the beauty of Orlando's soul in disguise. Phoebe is unable either to curb the Promethean fire of love that flashes in her eyes or to believe that they are shooting the ray of love from Cupid's dart into Silvius' heart:

> Lie not, to say mine eyes are murderers,
> Now show the wound mine eye hath made in thee . . .
>
> 3.5.19–20

To which Silvius replies that one day she may feel the wounds of love herself:

> O dear Phoebe,
> If ever, as that ever may be near,
> You meet in some fresh cheek the power of fancy,
> Then shall you know the wounds invisible
> That love's keen arrows make.
>
> 3.5.27–31

Her meeting with 'some fresh cheek' is imminent, for at that moment Rosalind steps forward to intervene in the lovers' quarrel and Phoebe's eyes flash with desire, giving Rosalind cause to exclaim:

> 'Od's my little life,
> I think she means to tangle my eyes too!
> 3.5.43–4

As soon as Rosalind drops her disguise, the veil of illusion also falls from Phoebe's eyes and she has no option but to recognise Silvius as her soul-mate. As Hymen conducts the wedding of all four couples, he speaks of the harmony of the soul. Love has brought the pairs of lovers together, evenly balanced in heavenly harmony and, with heaven and earth thus conjoined, their souls are in atonement, at-onement:

> Then is there mirth in heaven
> When earthly things made even
> Atone together.
> 5.4.107–9

CHAPTER THREE

The Goddess of Nature

———•·•———

I N THE PREVIOUS chapter we saw how the second step on the
path of love, after falling in love with physical beauty, is for the
lover to discover his own natural virtues. As a human being is a
microcosm of the universal world, so his body, heart (in its meaning
of soul) and mind reflect the body, soul and angelic mind of the macrocosm. Man's nature ornaments or disfigures his physical being in
the same way that the natural world clothes the earth. Similar forces
of nature operate on both scales; as nature erupts in a tempest, so our
natures erupt in temper. Shakespeare often uses the imagery of taming wild vegetation or a disordered garden to picture the taming of
personal nature or a disordered nation. In *Richard II,* the gardeners
sadly ruminate that the King has failed to cultivate his garden of the
kingdom as they do theirs:

> Why should we, in the compass of a pale,
> Keep law and form and due proportion,
> Showing, as in a model, our firm estate,
> When our sea-walled garden, the whole land,
> Is full of weeds, her fairs't flowers chok'd up,
> Her fruit-trees all unprun'd, her hedges ruin'd,
> Her knots disordered, and her wholesome herbs
> Swarming with caterpillars?
>
> 3.4.40–7

Both universal and personal nature is sometimes described by
Ficino as a fourth world but, when viewed as the ornament of all
the forms perceived by the senses, it becomes an essential part of the
physical world. As the last world to be created, the body receives its
nature by virtue of the soul, itself the recipient of God's love, and

nature, covering both earth and man, itself becomes the procreative power of the loving soul:

> When we say Nature, we mean the power placed in the Soul's faculty of procreation.[1]

Having lovingly formed the body of the world, nature ornaments it with its beauty and enables it to perform according to its laws. These laws are innate: it is in the nature of nature, for instance, that spring will follow winter and seeds will produce fruit. The human body is ornamented not only with its outward appearance but also with the inner nature of its whole being, both of which are essentially beautiful. The many references Shakespeare makes to nature may be appreciated in as many ways, but the deeper meaning lying behind his preoccupation with this subject is a revelation of how and why the original perfection of man's inner nature and his world should ever change and how it may be restored. During the course of Lady Macbeth's first scene in *Macbeth*, in which she conceives the idea of murdering the king, she uses the word 'nature' three times, and each time it has a very different connotation. At first, it is Macbeth's personal nature that she fears, his innate kindness:

> Yet do I fear thy nature:
> It is too full o'th'milk of human kindness,
> To catch the nearest way.
>
> 1.5.16–18

She then becomes anxious that her 'fell purpose' should be shaken by 'no compunctious visitings of Nature' (1.5.45–6), implying that there is a greater, more compassionate nature capable of pricking her conscience. Only five lines later she is still calling on the greater nature, but now its sound negates all love and mercy. Stemming from darkness, served by blind and murdering ministers, it reeks of evil:

> Come to my woman's breasts,
> And take my milk for gall, you murth'ring ministers,
> Wherever in your sightless substances
> You wait on Nature's mischief! Come, thick Night,
> And pall thee in the dunnest smoke of Hell . . .
>
> 1.5.47–51

Where he gives nature a gender, Shakespeare invariably refers to her as feminine and often as a goddess; but clearly it is important to understand which aspect of the goddess of nature is being invoked. Belarius, the guardian of Cymbeline's two young sons whom he has brought up in a cave, far from the royal palace of their birth, praises nature's love and magnanimity for bestowing an innate gentleness and royalty on the princes:

> Oh thou goddess,
> Thou divine Nature; thou thyself thou blazon'st
> In these two princely boys; they are as gentle
> As zephyrs blowing below the violet . . .
>
> 4.2.169–72

This is the compassionate goddess so feared by Lady Macbeth; but the goddess that Edmund calls upon in *King Lear* is very different:

> Thou, Nature, art my goddess; to thy law
> My services are bound.
>
> 1.2.1–2

She is the same dark deity invoked by Lady Macbeth. As a natural son, a bastard conceived 'in the lusty stealth of nature' (1.2.11), Edmund believes, like Lady Macbeth, that she will aid him in his fell purpose to destroy, not a king, but his own half-brother and his father's legitimate heir, Edgar.

Although this goddess, by whom Lady Macbeth wishes to be filled 'from the crown to the toe, top-full / Of direst cruelty' (1.5.42–3), seems to be far removed from the goddess holding the procreative power of love, she is in fact an aspect of the same divine nature who is addressed by Belarius. As the dark side of the goddess she is Hecate; hers is the uncreated nature of the body of the world, as yet unawakened by love. Her powers are unknown rather than evil but, because of her darkness and lack of form, she attracts the uglier side of human imagination. Those whose natures have lost contact with love fall under her sway.

In her darkness, too, lies lunacy. This word is derived from 'lunar', to do with the moon; hence the lunatic imagination, 'that sees more devils than vast hell can hold' (*Dream* 5.1.9), is dominated by Hecate, the dark side of the moon. While the period of the actual waning of the old moon is sometimes associated with her, the form of Hecate usually represents the period when the moon is unmanifest, between the waning of the old and the birth of the new:

> Now o'er the one half-world
> Nature seems dead, and wicked dreams abuse
> The curtain'd sleep: Witchcraft celebrates
> Pale Hecate's off'rings . . .
>
> *Macbeth* 2.1.49–52

The moon has long been recognised as a symbol of nature, the formative principle behind all matter that Hermes Tristmegisthus describes: 'See the moon. . . instrument of nature, transforming matter below'[2] and, both mythologically and according to the Platonic teaching, the planets are the physical bodies of the gods. So, as the form of the moon changes from a crescent to a fullness and finally wanes into darkness, it reveals the different faces of its three goddesses, collectively the triple goddess of nature. In the Greek myth, Demeter is the full moon, the goddess of the harvest and the abundance of nature, while her daughter, Persephone, represents the two other aspects of the goddess. During the months she spends in the underworld with Hades she shares the same dark aspect of nature as Hecate and, returning in the spring, she becomes, like Artemis, the virgin goddess of the new moon. In a later period the gods and their planets became known by their Roman names, which are those used by Shakespeare and which have continued to the present day.

Diana, with her curved bow of the new moon, is the goddess of virgin nature in all the beauty of its first creation, untouched by man. Orlando addresses the 'thrice-crowned queen of night' as he pins his verses on the forest trees in the first throes of love, but it is her particular aspect of Diana, with her 'chaste eye', whom he invokes, the pale sphere of the virgin moon goddess being, of course, the appropriate form for Rosalind:

> Hang there my verse, in witness of my love,
> And thou, thrice-crowned queen of night, survey
> With thy chaste eye, from thy pale sphere above,
> Thy huntress' name, that my full life doth sway.
>
> 3.2.1–4

She makes a rare appearance in her human form to Pericles, albeit in a dream; he hails her as 'Celestial Dian—goddess argentine' (5.1.248), a reference to her silvery moon-like appearance. Following her bidding to hasten to her temple at Ephesus, he is reunited there with his wife, Thaisa, whom he had for many years believed drowned. Diana has kept her as one of her chaste priestesses until, in her role as the heavenly part of his soul, Pericles is ready to receive her back.

The bounty of nature is personified by Ceres, goddess of the harvest and, in planetary form, the golden-red full moon. She appears as a character in the masque conjured up by Prospero in *The Tempest*, giving her blessing to the earth. Wishing that the rebirth of spring should be followed by a fruitful harvest, she banishes her sister Hecate, the wintry face of nature:

> Earth's increase, foison plenty,
> Barns and garners never empty;
> Vines with clust'ring bunches growing;
> Plants with goodly burthen bowing;
> Spring come to you at the farthest
> In the very end of harvest!
> Scarcity and want shall shun you;
> Ceres blessing so is on you.

4.1.110–17

The harvest cannot be produced without a harmonious partnership between man and nature and, for this reason, Ceres represents nature in her cultivated form. As Polixenes says in *The Winter's Tale*, it is the art of man as the gardener that 'does mend nature', although, he continues, 'the art itself is nature' (4.4.96–7)—that is, if the artistic result is to be fruitful and harmonious, he must abide by the laws of nature herself. This applies to the tending of his own nature, as well as his encouragement of growth for the well-being of the world.

The ultimate goal of all this horticulture is to re-establish the perfection of creation and to unite with the same perfection of its Creator. The means is first to discover the laws of nature and, in so doing, man may then discover him- or herself. Francis Bacon, Shakespeare's contemporary and quite possibly his philosophical teacher, believed that it is no use speculating about divine matters but that we should learn from what is in front of us, from nature herself, and find

'Following the Footsteps of Nature', from Michael Maier,
Atalanta fugiens, *Oppenheim, 1618*

our way back to God by 'following the footsteps of nature'. He argued
that, through close observation of nature, it is possible to trace back
to her root causes, to the laws by which she is held and operates in
creation:

> the springhead thereof seemeth to me not to have been visited;
> being of so excellent use, both for the disclosing of nature and the
> abridgment of art.[3]

The image of following nature's footsteps was common in contemporary thought and a popular book of the time shows an emblem of
a philosopher holding up a lantern that is lighting the way to truth.
Leaning on the staff of reason and bespectacled for greater vision, he is
following closely the footsteps of nature in her Ceres form; she herself
walks before him carrying fruit and flowers. Above her head may be
seen her symbol of the moon, depicted in its varying phases.

One of the natural laws that the philosopher may be trying to discover is that of proportion. Contained within her forms, this pleasing harmony is to be found throughout nature: the proportions of the golden mean, for instance, may be discovered on the coiled shell of a snail and between the veins of a leaf. Such proportions are held in the angelic world of the universal mind and, in the same way that nature uses them to create her many forms, so they may be employed by man in the creation of his art. If he follows these laws of proportion, the artist will be bringing the harmony of heavenly forms to those on earth. Plotinus, the third-century Platonist who had a considerable influence on Ficino, wrote the following on how the artist's imitation of nature leads us back to the essential forms lying in the highest world of the intellect:

> If anyone despises the arts because they produce their works by imitating nature, we must tell him, first, that natural things are imitations too. Then he must know that the arts do not simply imitate what they see, but they run back up to the forming principles from which nature derives.[4]

As a gardener, man is permitted to mend or even change nature, but only in accord with nature's own art. Hence Polixenes' response to Perdita in *A Winter's Tale*:

> Yet nature is made better by no mean
> But nature makes that mean: so over that art,
> Which you say adds to nature, is an art
> That nature makes. You see, sweet maid, we marry
> A gentler scion to the wildest stock,
> And make conceive a bark of baser kind
> By bud of nobler race. This is an art
> Which does mend nature—change it, rather—but
> The art itself is nature.
>
> 4.4.89–97

As the gardener of his own nature, man has the opportunity to tend it according to the laws of harmony, but if, on the other hand, he chooses to ignore natural law and create war, disorder and havoc in himself, it will reflect in the disruption of both heaven and earth. The binding force of love is forgotten and the chaos of Hecate takes over. At this moment of disharmony in his plays, when man's nature and his world are out of joint and tragedy is imminent, invariably there is an eruption of the gods in their planetary forms, complemented by strange portents and unnatural happenings in the natural world.

Hecate was also known as the goddess of the crossroads who appears when man, or nation, has reached a point of decision between good or ill. At a crossroads in his life, Macbeth encounters Hecate in the form of her servants, the three witches, thus becoming subject to her influence and a prey to his darker imaginings. This is the goddess whom Lady Macbeth has also invoked and, until redemption arrives with the death of both husband and wife, she continues to preside over the play. Although many critics believe the scenes in which she appears as an actual character are later additions and not by Shakespeare, her position as the dark side of Macbeth's nature justifies her appearance at the point when, shaken by Banquo's ghost, he foresees the continuation of his murderous path: 'We are yet but young in deed' (3.4.143).

When Hecate officiates there is, of course, no visible moon but, on the night of Duncan's murder, the starry forms of all the other gods also hide their lights: 'There's husbandry in heaven; their candles are all out' (2.1.4–5). As the gods are angry, all mayhem reigns in nature:

> The night has been unruly: where we lay,
> Our chimneys were blown down; and as they say,
> Lamentings heard i'th'air; strange screams of death,
> And, prophesying with accents terrible
> Of dire combustion, and confus'd events,
> New hatch'd to th'woeful time, the obscure bird
> Clamour'd the livelong night: some say, the earth
> Was feverous and did shake.
>
> 2.3.53–9

When the ghost first appears in *Hamlet,* Horatio recalls that it was a similar night when Caesar was murdered. Again there was no moon:

> the moist star,
> Upon whose influence Neptune's empire stands,
> Was sick almost to doomsday with eclipse.
>
> 1.1.121–3

Unnatural phenomena terrify in the streets and reflect the anger of the gods in cosmic pyrotechnics:

> The graves stood tenantless, and the sheeted dead
> Did squeak and gibber in the Roman streets;
> As stars with trains of fire and dews of blood,
> Disasters in the sun . . .
>
> 1.1.118–21

In *Julius Caesar* itself, as the senators plot the murder, the fearful Casca speaks of the unnatural happenings he has witnessed both in heaven and on earth. 'A tempest dropping fire' (1.3.10) from the heavens, is mirrored on the earth below by a slave who

> Held up his left hand, which did flame and burn
> Like twenty torches join'd; and yet his hand,
> Not sensible of fire, remain'd unscorch'd.
>
> 1.3.16–18

A lion with a glazed expression passes quietly down the street and an owl shrieks at midday in the market-place: both animal and bird, whose behaviour here is so against their natures, are emblems of Hecate.

From these portents, Casca deduces that men have been 'too saucy with the gods' (1.3.12), for it is in retaliation for man's misdemeanours that the gods display their rage in the heavens and disrupt the order of the natural world. Although Cassius persuades Casca that these portents are but warnings of what will happen if Caesar should become king, he does admit that the heavens are, in fact, reflecting the bloody business of Caesar's murder planned for that night:

> the complexion of the element
> In favour's like the work we have in hand,
> Most bloody, fiery, and most terrible.
>
> 1.3.128–30

Woe betide any unbeliever in heavenly portents! At the start of *King Lear*, Gloucester worries that 'These late eclipses in the sun and moon portend no good to us' (1.2.100). These are but mild heavenly phenomena compared with the wrathful storm that is to come. Although

Edmund mocks his superstition as 'the excellent foppery of the world' (115), he is still an avowed devotee of the dark goddess, caught up in 'a divine thrusting on' (123) of evil that will eventually be his undoing.

Hecate is the crone of winter, the season when the earth rests, and in the darkness of her womb seeds germinate in preparation for a new cycle of life. After the horrors and dark deeds of Macbeth, spring, like Persephone, returns from the underworld. At the death of Macbeth, a new moon arises in Malcolm, the potential hero and future king, who speaks of a hopeful future and the seeds of a new life, 'Which would be newly planted with the time' (5.9.31). In a measured way, he will punish the evil-doers and, by the grace of God, fulfil the duties of a good king:

> . . . this, and what needful else,
> That calls upon us, by the grace of Grace,
> We will perform in measure, time and place.
>
> 5.9.37–9

Similar figures of re-birth speak the last lines of other plays. With the death of Hamlet, Fortinbras arrives to begin a new dynasty in Denmark. As an unknown knight with his visor drawn, Edgar rises from the ravages of nature that he has undergone in the guise of Poor Tom to overcome the dark powers personified by his brother, Edmund, and to begin a new cycle as the king after the death of Lear. Richmond, who becomes the new king, Henry VII, after the death of Richard III at Bosworth Field, also emerges, phoenix-like, from the chaos of the old order to begin a new dynasty of the Tudors, enriched with 'smooth-fac'd peace. . . smiling plenty and fair prosperous days' (5.5.33–4). On the individual level, it is interesting to note that, before the Battle of Bosworth, the setting sun gives Richmond 'a token of a goodly day tomorrow' (5.3.21), whilst the absence of sun in the morning is seen by Richard as an omen of doom, 'A black day will it be to somebody' (5.3.281), and he seems to think it will be for him. Although, as Richard says, they share 'the self-same heaven' (5.3.287), each realises his own interpretation of the portents.

Like Lady Macbeth and Edmund, Lear deliberately invokes the dark aspect of the goddess and, as they do, pays the price. When Lear, angered by Cordelia's silence, summons the whole pantheon of gods to witness his rejection of her, he particularly mentions Hecate by name:

> For, by the sacred radiance of the sun,
> The mysteries of Hecate and the night,
> By all the operation of the orbs
> From whom we do exist and cease to be,
> Here I disclaim all my paternal care . . .
>
> 1.1.108–12

As his own nature is clouded in the darkness of his egotistical outburst, he fails to recognise Cordelia's loving nature and believes her to be 'a wretch whom Nature is ashamed to acknowledge hers' (1.1.211–12). This statement maligns not only Cordelia but also the protector of maidens, who happens to be the Diana aspect of the goddess of nature.

His next invocation to the goddess is in the form of a curse, and a very terrible one, when his eldest daughter, Goneril, is not as hospitable as he would like:

> Hear, Nature, hear! dear Goddess, hear!
> Suspend thy purpose, if thou didst intend
> To make this creature fruitful!
> Into her womb convey sterility!
> Dry up in her the organs of increase,
> And from her derogate body never spring
> A babe to honour her! If she must teem,
> Create her child of spleen, that it may live
> And be a thwart disnatur'd torment to her!
>
> 1.4.273–81

His invocation will have been heard by all three aspects of the goddess, for although his appeal is to Hecate as the destructive force, neither Diana, as goddess of childbirth, nor Ceres, the goddess of earth's increase, will take kindly to a father imposing such a terrible curse on his own daughter, however ungrateful he believes her to be.

Having so angrily invoked all three aspects of the goddess without sufficient cause, it is hardly surprising that he receives the brunt of nature's anger in return. Having been so disturbed on earth, nature and all the gods react together and, as the heavens break asunder, their own rage manifests in the greatest and most famous of all Shakespeare's storms. On being thrown into the chaotic darkness of Hecate, Lear collapses into lunacy. 'Oppressed nature sleeps' (3.6.95), observes Kent, as he nods off after his ordeal, in the shelter offered by Gloucester. For the storm also acts as a purge upon Lear. As he sleeps in the dark womb of Hecate, the impediments of Lear's nature are slowly destroyed and he is reborn as a child of nature. When next we meet the newly re-created Lear, he is dressed fantastically in wild flowers, emerging from the darkness as a very new moon in the untamed state of the goddess. His mind is still as wild as his physical condition: 'He was met even now', cries Cordelia to the doctor, 'As mad as the vexed sea.' She then lists, very specifically, the flowers with which he has crowned himself as those that grow wild: the untamed aspect of nature compared with that towards which he has yet to grow, the 'sustaining corn', as she says, of Ceres' harvest:

> Crown'd with rank fumiter and furrow weeds,
> With hardocks, hemlock, nettles, cuckoo-flowers,
> Darnel, and all the idle weeds that grow
> In our sustaining corn.
>
> 4.4.1–6

In this state, Lear is still experiencing the confused feelings from his past life, which makes Gloucester exclaim: 'O ruin'd piece of Nature!' (4.6.133). Explaining to Cordelia that the 'foster-nurse of nature is repose' (4.4.12), the doctor offers medicines to give Lear this necessary sleep. Thereupon, Cordelia calls upon Ceres, offering tears of love to water the earth for the speedy growth of medicinal herbs:

> All bless'd secrets,
> All you unpublish'd virtues of the earth,
> Spring with my tears! be aidant and remediate
> In the good man's distress.
>
> 4.4.15–18

However, Lear shows some wisdom in his madness. He understands that, while the impediments of his nature can be destroyed, the gifts with which he has been endowed by nature herself cannot. Born a king, he cannot have that divine right taken from him: 'I am the king himself,' he cries, 'Nature's above art in that respect' (4.6.84–6).

Nature's gifts are moulded from the seeds of her womb; 'Crack Nature's moulds,' cries Lear as the gods rage at the height of the storm and the many corporeal forms of nature seem to be disintegrating about him, 'all germens spill at once' (3.2.8). The magnitude of the storm suggests the simultaneous releasing of all potential germens or seed forms. Since nature is the procreative power of the Creator and her seeds are thought forms, she creates from these seeds both the physical seeds from which spring human, animal and vegetable forms and also the seeds of their own natures that dictate behaviour; in human beings these are the essential qualities that form our fundamental characters.

Nurtured by nature in her womb, like Cymbeline's young sons in their cave, it is then up to the human race, her gardeners, to cultivate or neglect the young plants, although it is impossible to change their innate qualities. 'How hard it is to hide the sparks of Nature' (3.3.79), worries Belarius. Although they were stolen from the court in their infancy and lack a princely upbringing, their uncultivated natures act according to the potential of their seed:

> 'Tis wonder
> That an invisible instinct should frame them
> To royalty unlearn'd, honour untaught,
> Civility not seen from other, valour
> That wildly grows in them, but yields a crop
> As if it had been sow'd.
>
> 4.2.176–81

Although Shakespeare writes of nature as feminine, the procreative force that carries seeds to the world of nature from their archetypal seed forms in the angelic mind has a masculine connotation. Duncan, the god-like king murdered by Macbeth, presents himself in this masculine role as the planter of seeds. In the first act he takes credit for having planted the seeds of Macbeth's heroic qualities:

> I have begun to plant thee, and will labour
> To make thee full of growing.
>
> 1.4.28–9

As his wife recognises, Macbeth is full of human kindness and has every potential to cultivate and harvest the seeds of love, beauty

and goodness with which he has been endowed by nature. A greater
significance is added to the king's murder when it is realised that
Duncan is the representative of the Godhead on earth, acting here as
the procreative power of God in nature.

The tragedy of Macbeth is that he does not tend his nature according
to nature's laws but rather breaks them, in a dramatic reversal of all that
is innate in his essential being. In fact, it is directly after his meeting
with Duncan that he rejects this opportunity for growth and reverts to
the dark path presented to him at the crossroads. He appeals to Hecate
and the powers of darkness:

> Stars, hide your fires!
> Let not light see my black and deep desires.
>
> 1.4.50–1

Banquo is also acknowledged by Duncan as having the same potential
but, unlike Macbeth, as he is enfolded in the king's embrace he declares
his intention to develop within the arms of nature, according to its
laws:

> There if I grow,
> The harvest is your own.
>
> 1.4.32–3

With his murder, Banquo is not given the chance to grow in this life,
but it is interesting that the new king, Malcolm, as the symbol of
rebirth at the end of the play, should use the same imagery of planting
that was quoted earlier for his new reign.

Apart from such allusions, neither the male aspect of nature nor
the name of Pan, traditionally the god of nature, is mentioned by
Shakespeare. However, while the poet dwells on nature in her feminine aspect, her wild, uncultivated virginity as Diana, her nurturing
qualities as the mother, Ceres, and her unformed or destructive power
as Hecate, the more cerebral Francis Bacon writes only of nature in
the masculine form of Pan, as the vehicle for the seeds of creation.
In his *Wisdom of the Ancients*,[5] Pan, 'the universal nature of all things',
is described as the son of Mercury, the messenger of the gods who,
in Christian terms, is the divine Word or the creative power of God.
While his father carries the ray of beauty from God that seeds the

higher worlds, Pan is the messenger who bears the seeds of nature to the body of the world and remains there, according to Bacon, as 'nature itself'. Bacon also describes Pan as 'confused matter', an apt name for the primeval chaos of Hecate.

Thus, while Shakespeare writes of the goddess and Bacon of Pan, the two not only complement one another but also help to further our understanding of each other's work. For instance Pan, Bacon tells us, wears horns because nature is forever surging heavenward so as to unite with the divine—a concept firmly rooted in Platonism:

> Horns are given him, broad at the roots, but narrow and sharp at the top, because the nature of all things seems pyramidal; for individuals are infinite, but being collected into a variety of species, they rise up into kinds, and these again ascend, and are contracted into generals, till at length nature may seem collected to a point.[6]

Shakespeare writes on this aspect of nature in *Macbeth*. As a change from the destructive powers of Hecate dwelt on throughout most of this play, he describes the Ceres aspect of 'bounteous Nature', who bestows the gifts of various natures on each species of animal, as she does on every individual human being. Each is given a 'particular addition', although all spring from One: 'the bill that writes them all alike'.

> . . . hounds, and greyhounds, mongrels, spaniels, curs,
> Shoughs, water-rugs, and demi-wolves, are clept
> All by the name of dogs: the valu'd file
> Distinguishes the swift, the slow, the subtle,
> The housekeeper, the hunter, every one
> According to the gift which bounteous Nature
> Hath in him clos'd; whereby he does receive
> Particular addition, from the bill
> That writes them all alike; and so of men.
>
> 3.1.92–100

One fancies that Shakespeare was struggling over his accounts at the time he was writing this for his imagery of 'catalogue', 'valu'd file' and 'particular addition from the bill that writes them all alike' makes nature sound like some sort of divine book-keeper!

As Bacon tells the myth, Pan is the loser in two contests. The first is a wrestling match with Cupid, the god of love. The victory of love over nature proves that love is not only stronger than nature, but that it is also the power by which nature is tamed and cultivated; we find, for instance, that it is the strength of Cordelia's love which eventually tames Lear's nature. The other contest depicts Pan as the harmony of nature that man aspires to cultivate in imitation of heavenly harmony. For this reason Pan is given a pipe with seven reeds, representing the seven harmonious planetary spheres. Proud of his playing, he has the audacity to challenge Apollo, god of heavenly harmony, to a musical contest which, of course, he loses. As earthly harmony cannot better the heavenly but only try to emulate it, Pan is rewarded with the ass's ears of ignorance!

In *The Golden Ass* of Apuleius, translated into English in 1566 and undoubtedly known to Shakespeare, Lucius, while sleeping, is given a vision of the goddess of nature not as the triple goddess but as Isis, whose worship the Romans had inherited from the Egyptians. Here the goddess of nature appears in the fullness of her being, her three aspects in one: 'I am Nature, the universal Mother, mistress of all the elements.'[7]

The ancient belief that if one could pierce the veil of Isis the mystery of life would be discovered, is comparable to Bacon's metaphor of following the footprints of nature in order to reveal the secrets of the universe. In the tangled web of the gods, Isis is also associated with the heavenly Venus, whom Ficino calls human nature, and it is in the terms of this elevated form of the goddess that he writes of its perfection, with a warning that it should not to be underrated:

> Venus. . . which is human nature. . . Beware that you never despise it, perhaps thinking that human nature is born of earth, for human nature herself is a nymph with body surpassing. She was born of an heavenly origin and was beloved above others by an ethereal god. For indeed, her soul and spirit are love and kinship; her eyes are majesty and magnanimity; her hands are liberality and greatness in action; her feet, gentleness and restraint. Finally, her whole is harmony and integrity, honour and radiance.[8]

This is Shakespeare's goddess of divine Nature, whose qualities were blazoned in the sons of Cymbeline. She is also the goddess of love for it is through the love of the nature of beauty that man can come to appreciate that his own nature is indeed as Ficino describes.

CHAPTER FOUR

A Woman Mov'd

———••———

ONE OF SHAKESPEARE'S earliest plays, *The Taming of the Shrew*, contains a scene of such contention for feminists that some women actors have refused to play the part of Katherine. During the marriage feast at the end of the play, the three newly wed wives, Kate, her sister, Bianca, and the Widow, have left the room; Petruchio then demonstrates his wife's obedience by wagering with the other husbands that his wife will be the one to respond most quickly to her husband's call. Whilst the other wives send their excuses, Kate wins the wager for him by appearing directly. On Petruchio's orders she fetches the women and further demonstrates her obedience when he asks her to remove her cap and trample it underfoot. She follows this up with a long speech in which she rebukes the other wives for their lack of humility and submission:

> Fie, fie! Unknit that threatening unkind brow,
> And dart not scornful glances with those eyes,
> To wound thy lord, thy king, thy governor.
> It blots thy beauty as frosts do bite the meads,
> Confounds thy fame as whirlwinds shake fair buds,
> And in no sense is meet or amiable.
> A woman mov'd is like a fountain troubled,
> Muddy, ill-seeming, thick, bereft of beauty,
> And while it is so, none so dry or thirsty
> Will deign to sip or touch one drop of it.
> Thy husband is thy lord, thy life, thy keeper,
> Thy head, thy sovereign; one that cares for thee,
> And for thy maintenance; commits his body
> To painful labour both by sea and land,
> To watch the night in storms, the day in cold,
> Whilst thou liest warm at home, secure and safe;
> And craves no other tribute at thy hands
> But love, fair looks, and true obedience;
> Too little payment for so great a debt.

> Such duty as the subject owes the prince
> Even such a woman oweth to her husband.

She continues in this vein until, to demonstrate her allegiance, she offers to place her hand beneath his foot:

> In token of which duty, if he please,
> My hand is ready, may it do him ease.
>
> 5.2.137–80

Directors and actors have contrived over recent years to overcome this apparent indignity to women through many imposed interpretations, from tongue-in-cheek mockery on Kate's part to sadistic terrorism on Petruchio's, but the true significance of the scene is seldom realised.

The Taming of the Shrew is an early play, quite possibly the first that Shakespeare wrote concerning the ascent of the soul. In most of the comedies, once the lover discovers in which lady his soul lies and is caught by the beauty of her appearance, his first step is to discover her virtues. This play differs in that Kate is no tutelary Rosalind and Petruchio is given no help from the soul herself; also, before he can begin to love either beauty of form or beauty of virtue, he has to deal with the basic problem of bringing his unruly nature under control. It was shown in the last chapter how Shakespeare encompassed the universal aspect of nature from its divine perfection to its disruption into the chaos of abnormal occurrences on earth. In *The Taming of the Shrew*, we are presented with disruptive nature in the lower part of Petruchio's soul. Since the personification of a man's soul is a woman, the nature of the soul out of harmony with itself is rightly embodied as a shrew, a term still current in Shakespeare's time for a woman given to railing or scolding.

Petruchio, a soldier and adventurer, descends on Padua with all the unleashed energy of universal nature:

> Have I not in my time heard lions roar?
> Have I not heard the sea, puff'd up with winds,
> Rage like an angry boar chafed with sweat?
> Have I not heard great ordnance in the field,
> And heaven's artillery thunder in the skies?
>
> 1.2.199–203

Petruchio has come to Padua in search of a wife and, on being presented with Katherina, the rich but shrewish daughter of his father's friend, Baptista Minola, he recognises his own unruly nature in this wild young woman. At the same time, he receives the right signals for the true lover when Kate's beauty, and the light whereby he sees it, awaken him to the knowledge that she is his soul-mate:

> For by this light, whereby I see thy beauty,
> Thy beauty that doth make me like thee well,
> Thou must be married to no man but me.
>
> 2.1.266–8

His wooing is a mixture of bawdy ribaldry, as befits the coarseness of man's lower nature, and what she believes to be ironic mockery:

> Hearing thy mildness prais'd in every town,
> Thy virtues spoke of, and thy beauty sounded,
> Yet not so deeply as to thee belongs,
> Myself am mov'd to woo thee for my wife.
>
> 2.1.191–4

Although contrary to her behaviour and appearance, Petruchio is speaking truthfully, for the soul *is* beautiful and virtuous, as indeed is Kate, although, both as herself and as his soul, she has yet to realise that fact.

Having been wooed against her will, the wedding day is set and Kate reluctantly awaits her bridegroom. But Petruchio is about to begin the curbing of unruly nature with a method of deprivation: what dissatisfied nature expects and thinks it needs, it will not get. Thus Katherine, assuming the punctual arrival of a well-dressed bridegroom, is left waiting at the church; Petruchio, when he finally arrives, is arrayed in a ridiculous collection of old and ill-matching garments, his horse and servant as laughably caparisoned. Once the ceremony has been performed, Kate's humiliation continues since, instead of attending the wedding feast at her father's house, Petruchio insists that they return immediately to his own home. As nature angrily asserts herself, Petruchio commands mastery of his disorderly soul:

> Nay, look not big, nor stamp, nor stare, nor fret;
> I will be master of what is mine own.

> She is my goods, my chattels, she is my house,
> My household stuff, my field, my barn,
> My horse, my ox, my ass, my any thing,
> And here she stands.

3.2.226–31

Their journey home becomes a mortification of the physical body. After falling under her horse in a bog, Kate manages to wade through the mud in time to save Petruchio's servant from the blows of his master, angry that he allowed the horse to stumble. The horses escape and the newly wedded wife arrives at her husband's house on foot, exhausted and cold, filthy and wet.

Railing at his servants, since those who serve his physical needs in his home may also be seen as the senses serving the body, he allows his mundane nature no satisfaction. Using the same trick of raising and then dashing her expectations, he constantly thwarts her desire for any form of physical comfort. After calling for a bowl of water so that Kate may wash herself, he knocks it from the servant's hands and, when at last food arrives for the ravenous Kate, he throws it to the floor declaring it to be burnt. Exhausted, she is finally allowed to go bed, but Petruchio sends the bedclothes flying, thus ensuring that she spends the night shivering with cold. He has now withdrawn all the basic needs of cleanliness, food, sleep and warmth, without which all natural creatures must die; however, although at this point it is hard to believe, he does it all for love, 'That all is done in reverent care of her' (4.1.191), as he tells the audience.

There is still far to go before turbulent nature comes under the control of its master and both the body and the mind of the soul are united, so when they retire to bed on their wedding night it is impossible for their marriage to be consummated. As far as the drama is concerned, although Kate may have expected to be deprived of sleep that night, it turns out not to be for sexual reasons but, on the contrary, because Petruchio keeps her awake by pretending to rail and curse against lustful incontinence. The real reason is, of course, that there can be no love-making until the marriage of the soul is complete.

When Petruchio explains his intentions to the audience it is interesting that, while he still refers to Kate as a shrew, he begins his speech by comparing her with a falcon:

My falcon now is sharp and passing empty,
And till she stoop she must not be full-gorg'd.

4.1.177–8

A shrew being a small earth-bound animal and a falcon a creature of
the air, it appears as if some elemental progress is beginning to take
place within the soul. The mud and rain she endures on their journey
represent the two earthly elements, while the falcon indicates a movement towards the more heavenly region of air, the region ruled by Juno
where the soul may come in contact with the angelic mind.

With the sensual world more or less under control, Petruchio
progresses to the adornment of nature, or rather he provides further
rebuffs to Kate's expectation of being well dressed. He calls for a tailor and a haberdasher so that Kate may be provided with fine clothes
for their return to her father's home. They bring caps and gowns on
which she seizes eagerly, but Petruchio continues his ploy of finding
fault and, against all her protestations, he declares them ill fitting and
poorly made. There is nothing but for her to return home in the simple
garments she is wearing:

> Well, come, my Kate, we will unto your father's
> Even in these honest mean habiliments.
> Our purses shall be proud, our garments poor,
> For 'tis the mind that makes the body rich,
> And as the sun breaks through the darkest clouds,
> So honour peereth in the meanest habit.
> What, is the jay more precious than the lark
> Because his feathers are more beautiful?
> Or the adder better than the eel
> Because his painted skin contents the eye?

4.3.166–75

There is a certain familiarity about these lines, that 'the outward shows
be not themselves'.[1] It is the mind that makes the body rich; the soul,
if she is simply clad in all her natural beauty, may learn what it is to be
known by the light of the mind. She may also know her own beauty
and for this her mind must be in accord with the divine mind. The
point where the highest part of the soul meets the heavenly world has
been reached and so the last lesson Petruchio needs to teach Kate is to

bring her mind into such total agreement with his own that they are in truth of one mind.

This lesson takes place in one of the most amusing scenes of the play. As Kate and Petruchio travel back to her home on the last steps of the soul's journey, he persuades her to agree with everything he says, however absurd. Worn out and anxious to keep the peace at all costs, she affirms that the sun is the moon and even, to an old man's amazement, that he is a 'Young budding virgin, fair, and fresh, and sweet' (4.5.36). The incongruity of it all provides some perfect comedic moments, but at the same time Shakespeare is demonstrating how the higher mind is able to see through the shadow of external appearances. The elemental progression is also indicated by their emergence into 'the sun that shines so bright' (4.5.5), the fire of the mind.

And so they return to her 'father's house', a Christian rather than a Platonic image of the heavenly world. Before they enter it, Petruchio asks her for a kiss, 'Kiss me Kate' (5.1.131). Although at first reluctant to give so open a show of her affection, she does kiss him and calls him 'love'. This is the first acknowledgement of their love and a proof that Petruchio has won his soul.

Now the wedding feast with which this chapter began can take place and Kate's behaviour and speech may be seen in a new light. If, for instance, one substitutes 'soul' for 'woman' in the line 'A woman mov'd is like a fountain troubled' (5.2.143), it is seen that a constantly vacillating soul must be one that is out of harmony with itself. The importance of a constant and unmoving soul will be discussed further in a later chapter, but it has already become clear that, when the nature of a soul is unruly, the gods are angry and respond with flying tempers in the microcosm and, in the macrocosm, tempests and other eruptions of the heavens. It is important that a man has mastery over his soul and protects it, for the soul's part is, as Kate can now say, to 'serve, love and obey' (5.2.165).

The cap that Petruchio orders Kate to remove and trample underfoot now becomes a symbol of the highest point of the soul where it is in complete union with the heavenly world; thus, in this gesture, heaven is brought to earth. Finally, after Kate's speech, they are free to bid the others goodnight and retire at long last to consummate their marriage, not only in their physical love but also in the greater union of soul and mind.

CHAPTER FIVE

Drowsy with the Harmony

And when Love speaks, the voice of all the gods
Make heaven drowsy with the harmony.

4.3.340–41

———•◆•———

T HIS QUOTATION from Berowne's long speech on love
in *Love's Labours Lost* poses the intriguing question of why,
when love speaks, should heaven become drowsy? One
might expect such a love to awaken heaven, setting the stars dancing rather than sending them to sleep. It is, however, divine love that
speaks, and this harmonious lullaby has a specific function in the ascent
of Platonic love.

The reflection of heavenly beauty on earth that we perceive through
our senses is also a reflection of heavenly harmony, for beauty is harmony. In the body of the world, it is found in both the harmony of
nature and in man's re-creation of the natural laws of harmonious
proportion through the cultivation of nature and the arts. Harmonic
proportions are held as ideas in the angelic mind and in the earthly
world as forms and sounds. Therefore the whole beauty of creation,
that includes the beauty of the human body, soul and mind, is the
natural reflection of heavenly beauty with which, in its perfect state,
it is in harmony. It is only through man's desires for beauty becoming
impure, distorted for instance by lust or greed, that, as Shakespeare
describes in *Macbeth*, *Lear* and other plays mentioned in Chapter 3,
the natural harmony between heaven and earth is disrupted. For this
reason only man himself can redress the balance.

To create harmony within himself and in the world around him,
man needs to seek and love first the beauty of form and then the beauty
of virtue, the theme of Shakespeare's comedies that was covered in
Chapter 2. It is only when he has achieved this that he is ready for
marriage with the higher part of his soul; Romeo and Juliet, Bassanio

and Portia, Orlando and Rosalind have, through their love, brought the beauty of heavenly virtue and the beauty of the earthly parts of their souls together in harmony.

Many of the court masques are in honour of an actual wedding union—such as *Hymenaei,* the staging of which was described in the first chapter—which was written to celebrate the marriage of the Earl of Essex and Lady Frances Howard. Although they contain many references to an historical union between England and Scotland, which at that time was eagerly desired by James I, now the king of both countries, the major theme of Jonson and Jones' masques is the union between heaven and earth and the path of man's ascent of love to union with God. With the attempt to create heavenly harmony on earth through the music, dance, poetry and visual beauty of the masque, the moment of union was traditionally represented by the masquers joining with members of the audience in a final dance before the king, the symbolic godhead. The dance in *Hymenaei* is supervised by Order, a character who, personifying harmonious proportion, wears a costume covered with mathematical figures. Reason, who appeared on top of the physical world in the setting, pointing the way to the world of the soul, now calls on the gentlemen to dance with the ladies. Having proved themselves sufficiently virtuous to enter the world of the soul, they join hands with the ladies, the beauty of their heavenly souls, to make a chain symbolising the golden chain that Platonists said linked the worlds in love and harmony. Here is yet another representation of the ray of divine light, the fire of love that lights the beauty of all the worlds. Reason continues with a description of the union of heaven and earth in the soul:

> Such was the golden chain let down from Heaven;
> And not those links more even,
> Than these: so sweetly temper'd, so combin'd
> By Union: and refin'd.
> Here no contention, envy, grief, deceit,
> Fear, jealousy have weight;
> But all is peace, and love, and faith, and bliss:
> What harmony like this?[1]

The union of the masquers taking the parts of the bride and groom is performed by Hymen, the god of marriage, who also presides at the wedding in *As You Like It.*

The idea of dancing as a symbol of union and harmony between heaven and earth is developed in the work of many other Renaissance poets. Sir John Davies, a contemporary of Shakespeare's, wrote a long poem on the subject, *Orchestra or a Poem of Dancing*. Here, Davies is describing how dancing springs from love and is, itself, love and harmony. As the archetypes of everything in creation are held in the angelic mind, so the 'true figures' of dance, he concludes, lie in heaven and, through the art of their performance, their heavenly beauty is drawn to the earth:

> Lo, this is Dancing's true nobility.
> Dancing the child of Music and of Love,
> Dancing itself both love and harmony,
> Where all agree, and all in order move;
> Dancing the Art that all Arts do approve:
> The fair character of the world's consent,
> The heav'ns true figure, and th'earth's ornament.[2]

Thus we often find that, whenever there is a wedding, Shakespeare provides his actors with a dance. 'We'll have dancing afterwards', cries Beatrice's uncle at her wedding with Benedick in *Much Ado About Nothing* (5.4.119), while Duke Senior calls for a dance after witnessing the marriage of his daughter, Rosalind, and the other couples in *As You Like It*. When Oberon and Titania are reconciled after her adventures with Bottom, Oberon calls first for music that will lull Bottom into a charmed sleep:

> Titania, music call; and strike more dead
> Than common sleep, of all these five the sense.

Soft music is played and then Oberon calls again for music, this time for a dance to celebrate both their own reunion and that of the lovers, who will shortly awake, to find their rightful partners beside them:

> Sound music!
> Come my queen, take hands with me
> And rock the ground whereon these sleepers be.
> Now thou and I are new in amity,
> And will tomorrow midnight, solemnly,
> Dance in Duke Theseus' house triumphantly,

And bless it to all prosperity,
There shall the pairs of faithful lovers be
Wedded, with Theseus, all in jollity.

4.1.80–91

Even where it is not specifically called for in the text, most modern stage productions of the comedies tend to end with a dance, sending their audiences out happily exhilarated that a harmonious conclusion has been reached.

In his *Masque of Beauty*, Jonson writes of the harmonious quality of the soul as 'the world's soul, true harmony'[3] and Inigo Jones' set for *Hymenaei* also signifies the soul as the place of harmony by placing the court ladies at the centre of the three worlds, surrounded by the harmonious presence of musicians. Ficino refers to Plato's *Phaedrus* when he is explaining how earthly harmony reflects the heavenly in the same way that wisdom and beauty of appearance are but images of divine wisdom and beauty:

> Plato says that the wisdom of men is the image of divine wisdom. He thinks that the harmony which we make with musical instruments and voices is the image of divine harmony, and that the symmetry and comeliness that arise from the perfect union of the parts and members of the body are an image of divine beauty.[4]

The Masque of Beauty presents a whole scene depicting the world of the soul. Again it is inhabited by the court ladies seated, as Jonson describes, on a 'throne of beauty'. The divine ray makes its appearance again, this time very obviously, as 'a translucent pillar, shining with several coloured lights', and the harmony of the soul is represented by a figure of the goddess, Harmonia. She holds a lyre and, in a like manner to Order who ushers the dancers into a harmonious dance in *Hymenaei*, she wears 'a robe painted full of figures'.[5] Because the soul is continually drawn in two directions at once, towards heaven and earth, Inigo Jones provided what must have been a dramatic sight for the audience, and a bone-shaking experience for the lady masquers. The throne stood on an island and the full ingenuity of Jacobean stage machinery came into action as a series of rollers caused it to move slowly across the water towards the audience. At the same time, the throne itself revolved in one direction 'ad motum mundi', in the

Costume design for Harmonia by Inigo Jones,
Tempe Restored, *1632*

direction of the world, while the steps upon which it was placed moved in the other, 'ad motum planetarum', according to the motion of the planets or the heavens.

Harmonia's crown contains seven jewels, representing the seven known planets at that time, whose movements are said to produce the music of the spheres. Like the two forms of Cupid and Venus, Ficino writes of two forms of harmony. Again one is divine, existing only in the mind of God, while the other is produced by the incarnate bodies of the gods as they move across the sky:

> According to the followers of Plato, divine music is twofold. One kind, they say, exists entirely in the eternal mind of God. The second is in the motions and order of the heavens, by which the heavenly spheres and their orbits make a marvellous harmony.[6]

This second harmony is the sound of which Berowne is speaking, 'the voice of all the gods', singing in tune with the soul.

In their highest form, the gods are the great archetypes of creation. Two of the creative forces, the word of God and the love of God, are represented in the Greek pantheon by Mercury and the heavenly Cupid, while Venus tends more towards the power or beauty of love. Apollo, meaning 'not many', is the fount of harmony. As such, he also represents the light of God whose physical form is the sun, with which Romeo compares Juliet. Thus the light that enters the soul of Romeo or any lover will also bring it into harmony. Plato speaks of Apollo as an active force:

> . . . the meaning of the name Apollo will be 'moving together', whether in the poles of heaven as they are called, or in the harmony of song, which is termed concord, because he moves altogether by an harmonious power, as astronomers and musicians ingeniously declare. And he is the god who presides over harmony, and makes all things move together, both among gods and among men.[7]

In one of his letters Ficino explains that once, before we were born, we knew this harmony, but now that we are confined in our mortal bodies we can no longer hear the voice of the gods. However, by listening to its reflection in earthly music, it is possible to be led back to a remembrance of what the soul once knew,

... before it was imprisoned in our bodies. But it uses the ears as messengers, as though they were chinks in this darkness. By the ears ... the soul receives the echoes of that incomparable music, by which it is led back to the deep and silent memory of the harmony which it previously enjoyed.[8]

In *The Merchant of Venice*, Lorenzo and Jessica have been left in charge of Portia's house at Belmont, a name meaning the mount of beauty which, like the throne of beauty in Jonson and Jones' masque, is a symbol of the soul. Shakespeare's imagery is akin to Ficino's when, as lovers entering this world in the starlit garden of Belmont, Lorenzo and Jessica are on the verge of hearing the harmony of heaven:

> There's not the smallest orb which thou behold'st
> But in his motion like an angel sings,
> Still choiring to the young-eyed cherubins.
> Such harmony is in immortal souls.
> But whilst this muddy vesture of decay
> Doth grossly close it in, we cannot hear it.
>
> 5.1.60–5

Shakespeare seems to be echoing Ficino's idea that, whilst imprisoned in the mortal body, we cannot hear the music of the immortals. Ficino continues his letter by explaining that in this condition the only way to hear the music of the spheres is by trying to imitate it:

> It [the soul] realises that as long as it is enclosed in the dark abode of the body it can in no way reach that music. It therefore strives wholeheartedly to imitate it.[9]

And so, as Lorenzo is explaining the difficulties of hearing the divine music, musicians enter and he calls on them to play. If they play sweetly enough, the music of the gods will be heard and their harmony will bring heaven to earth. He identifies Jessica with Diana, the chaste goddess of the moon, and asks for her to be awakened to the sound of the heavenly music so that, when it pierces her ears, which Ficino calls the 'chinks in the darkness', she will be drawn to the divine source itself, the 'home' of all music:

Come, ho, and wake Diana with a hymn,
With sweetest touches pierce your mistress' ear
And draw her home with music.

5.1.66–8

The main thrust of the comedies is towards harmony but, as the chapter on nature showed, Shakespeare's tragedies explore the lack of harmony in and among nations and the souls of their rulers. Whereas discord between heaven and earth continues throughout *Macbeth*, culminating in the battle in which Macbeth dies, by the end of *King Lear* the two worlds have begun to reunite. When Lear reaches the peak of his inner conflict, the disruption of harmony is reflected in the gigantic force of the storm on earth as the anger of the great gods thunders in heaven. This symbolic split between heaven and earth begins when Lear first divides his kingdom, thereby dividing both the unity of his nation and the kingdom of his own being. With promises of a share of his kingdom, Lear forces declarations of spurious love from his elder daughters, Goneril and Regan, and refuses to recognise the only true love offered to him by his third daughter, Cordelia. By banishing Cordelia from his kingdom, he banishes love from his life and loses the higher part of his soul. Having rejected so much, he in turn is rejected by his other daughters and is gradually reduced to 'a poor, bare, forked animal' (3.4.105–6). On the universal scale, there is further division between his sons-in-law, Albany and Cornwall, and the kingdom is scattered. Until Cordelia returns to England's shores the conflicts multiply, for she is not only the soul of the king, her father, but also the soul of the kingdom and while she is away there can be no concord.

After his ordeal in the wilderness, Lear awakes from a long sleep to find the loving Cordelia at his side, his soul restored to him once more. Their reunion is marked, as such moments invariably are by Shakespeare, with the sound of music signifying the return of harmony to the soul. 'Louder the music there!' calls the Doctor (4.7.25) and, as the restorative power of the music takes its effect, Lear is granted a brief period of harmony, a glimpse of heaven perhaps, before he dies, heartbroken by the death of Cordelia.

Shakespeare's last great romances, as they are often known, all have father and daughter relationships in common. In *The Tempest* because, like Cordelia's, her mother is dead, Prospero's daughter, Miranda, plays the part of her father's soul throughout the play. The same symbolic role is played by Imogen in *Cymbeline*. However, in *The Winter's Tale*, discussed more fully in Chapter 13, and *Pericles*, the daughters are but temporary custodians. Pericles and his family are tempest-tossed and his misfortunes find him out of harmony with the rest of the world. After her mother's apparent death at sea, he leaves their daughter, Marina, in the care of a foreign king. Kind, beautiful and accomplished, she represents her father's soul in exile and plays an active role in the preservation of its purity. Captured by pirates, she falls into evil hands but, because of her goodness and sweetness of nature, she manages to preserve her chastity. When she finds a husband the soul of Pericles is brought to maturity and, after many trials and tribulations, he is ready for its return. Believing both his wife and daughter to be dead, he lapses into a state of depressed lethargy and eventually arrives in the town where Marina is living. Little knowing that she is his daughter, Pericles' attendants introduce her as a singer to cheer him 'with her sweet harmony' (5.1.44). Slowly he discovers her true identity and, overjoyed, he embraces her. With this reunion he hears music that no others can hear, for it is the heavenly music only to be heard by those who have that harmony in their soul.

> PERICLES: But what music?
> HELICANUS: My lord, I hear none.
> PERICLES: None?
> The music of the spheres. List, my Marina.
> LYSIMACHUS: It is not good to cross him; give him way.
> PERICLES: Rarest sounds! Do ye not hear?
> LYSIMACHUS: Music, my lord, I hear.
> PERICLES: Most heavenly music!
> It nips me unto list'ning, and thick slumber
> Hangs upon mine eyes.
>
> 5.2.225–33

As he sleeps, Diana, the virgin goddess who has kept both his wife and daughter safe all these years, appears to him in a vision and directs him to her temple where Thaisa, his wife and his heavenly soul, has been preserved as a priestess. In the joy of their reunion, Marina, who

The Temple of Diana, design for Florimene *by Inigo Jones, 1635*

for so long has preserved her father's soul, now releases it back to her mother, its true owner:

> My heart
> Leaps to be gone into my mother's bosom.
>
> 5.3.44–5

Whenever heavenly harmony is heard, sleep seems to be near. As the music of the spheres arrests Pericles and 'nips him into listening', a 'thick slumber hangs' upon his eyes. Tuning to the voice of the goddess and the harmony of the soul, the physical world of his senses is stilled. This now begins to make a little more sense of the drowsiness spoken of by Berowne in the quotation at the beginning of this chapter.

> And when Love speaks, the voice of all the gods
> Make heaven drowsy with the harmony.

When the soul is awakened the body is lulled into drowsiness. The soul, united with its heavenly counterpart, is opened to the world of the angelic mind, and the music of the gods is heard, calming all discordance in the lower world. It is to this harmony of the soul that all true lovers aspire. When they are able to hear the voice of all the gods in the music of the spheres, they are listening to the voice of divine love itself.

However, many obstacles are set in the path of the lover before he can enter that heavenly world of the angelic mind. During the course of *Love's Labours Lost* there has been much merriment before the lovers are dismissed for their year of study. If they return, no doubt wiser and better, there will be a great deal of music to celebrate their marriages and Apollo, the god of harmony, will be honoured with singing and dancing. But it is Mercury, the messenger of the gods, who in his highest form is the word of God, that beckons them towards the world of the angelic mind. He arrives as Marcade, a similar name to Mercury, a messenger bearing the news that the father of the Princess is dead. Thus it is on a serious, even a harsh note that, with the final line of the play, the lovers are given an insight into the further stages of their spiritual journey:

The words of Mercury are harsh after the songs of Apollo.

CHAPTER SIX

Fancy and Imagination

———•◦•———

THE WORDS of Mercury may appear harsh, as the last line in *Love's Labours Lost* suggests, but they spring from the angelic mind and are given form by the creative imagination. Ficino called Mercury 'angelic inspiration'.[1] Inspiration fires the imagination and it is through imagination that it is possible to enter the world of the gods or, in other words, to experience and act from the higher mind. As an inspired poet, Shakespeare is able to write from first-hand knowledge of this world.

Ficino wrote to a young poet, Peregrino Agli, that such is the lover's burning desire for divine beauty it becomes a kind of madness. Having seen the reflection of divine beauty and heard the resonance of divine harmony, the lover's memory of what he has once known is fired and he 'becomes wholly possessed by divine frenzy'.[2] It was this frenzy that drove Romeo over the orchard walls, but it is also a frenzy that possesses a true poet like Shakespeare and drives him to express the divine beauty he sees through his inspired imagination.

The potential for all forms and all ideas arises from the mind of God and lies as seeds in the imagination. Creative imagination is the tool of divine consciousness, through which all that belongs to the lower worlds is created. Mankind, born in the image of God—that is, in His imagination—possesses the same creative imagination through which he can create on the human scale. In the *Corpus Hermeticum* of Hermes Tristmegistus, from which stems much of Ficino's philosophy, is a description of how God, the unmanifest, creates through imagination:

> That which makes manifest is not itself made manifest. . . but it brings all images to the mind in imagination. Things that are begot-

ten belong only to the imagination. For imagination is nothing but begetting.[3]

The imagination is given inspiration, meaning the breath of life, through the medium of the Muses whom Ficino, quoting Plato, calls the divine songs of the spheres. As we found in the chapter on harmony, these are the voices of all the gods, so whether they are called the Muses, or Apollo, or Mercury, they are instrumental in bringing the power of creative expression to those who are ready to receive it and inspiring them with divine frenzy. Ficino will often refer to God the Creator as Jove, as he does in the continuation of his letter to Peregrino Agli:

> poetry springs from divine frenzy, frenzy from the Muses, and the Muses from Jove.[4]

Thus, through inspiration received through the powers of the Muses, man may create with the imagination of God.

The Platonists related the element of fire to the angelic world and, when inspiration strikes the mind of the poet, it is the same Promethean fire that pierces the heart of the lover through the fiery dart of Cupid. This creative ray of light springing from the mind of God illumines the mind of man and gives inspiration to his creative imagination. So when, in the lines he gives to the Chorus at the start of *Henry V*, Shakespeare invokes the muse of fire, he is inviting inspiration not only from the furthest heaven of the angelic world, but also from the divine ray that circles through creation, descending from and ascending to the One:

> O for a muse of fire, that would ascend
> The brightest heaven of invention . . .

This is imagination at its highest level, but in *A Midsummer Night's Dream* Shakespeare shows how images of the angelic world that enter the mind of man in his imagination are easily dismissed, by those who consider themselves to be reasonable, as fancy and fantasy. When Hippolyta comments that the story of the lovers' night in the Athenian wood is strange, she provokes amused disbelief from Theseus that there may be any truth in their story. Through his love for Hippolyta,

Theseus is becoming acquainted with the world of the soul, but as yet he has had no experience of the angelic world of the imagination. Plato, in the *Phaedrus*,[5] says that two forms of madness are love and possession by the Muses resulting in poetry, so although his answer is within the Platonic context, it is at the level of 'cool reason' which, Theseus says himself, cannot comprehend the imaginative world. It will be remembered from Inigo Jones' stage design that reason controls, while still being part of the physical world:

> More strange than true. I never may believe
> These antique fables, nor these fairy toys.
> Lovers and madmen have such seething brains,
> Such shaping fantasies, that apprehend
> More than cool reason ever comprehends.
> The lunatic, the lover and the poet
> Are of imagination all compact:
> One sees more devils than vast hell can hold;
> That is the madman: the lover, all as frantic,
> Sees Helen's beauty in a brow of Egypt:
> The poet's eye, in a fine frenzy rolling,
> Doth glance from heaven to earth, from earth to heaven;
> And as imagination bodies forth
> The forms of things unknown, the poet's pen
> Turns them to shapes, and gives to airy nothing
> A local habitation and a name.
> Such tricks hath strong imagination,
> That if it would but apprehend some joy,
> It comprehends some bringer of that joy:
> Or, in the night, imagining some fear,
> How easy is a bush suppos'd a bear!

                                        5.1.2–22

Theseus speaks truly when he says that the lover sees Helen's beauty in a brow of Egypt, for he is speaking of the lover awakened by the glimpse of heavenly beauty in a physical body. And, as the poet's eye rolls in a fine frenzy between heaven and earth, he is describing the divine frenzy that is brought from heaven to earth by the Muses, bringing form to the creations of the imagination. But he fails to distinguish between true creative imagination, that can give form to things that are unknown to the physical world until they are made manifest, and fantasy that is entirely connected to the material world of the senses and performs such tricks of the lower mind as mistaking a bush for a bear.

Early in the nineteenth century, the poet Coleridge, himself both a Platonist and a Shakespearean critic, wrote these definitions of the imagination of God and man, and fancy:

> The IMAGINATION then I consider either as primary or secondary. The primary IMAGINATION I hold to be the living Power and prime Agent of all human Perception, and as a repetition in the finite mind of the eternal act of creation in the infinite I AM. The secondary I consider as an echo of the former, co-existing with the conscious will, yet still as identical with the primary in the *kind* of its agency, and differing only in *degree,* and in the *mode* of its operation. It dissolves, diffuses, dissipates, in order to re-create; or where this process is rendered impossible, yet still at all events it struggles to idealise and to unify. It is essentially *vital*, even as all objects (*as* objects) are essentially fixed and dead.
>
> FANCY, on the contrary, has no other counters to play with, but fixities and definites. The Fancy is indeed no other than a mode of Memory emancipated from the order of time and space; and blended with, and modified by that empirical phenomenon of the will, which we express by the word CHOICE. But equally with the ordinary memory it must receive all its materials ready made from the law of association.[6]

In *The Merchant of Venice*, as Bassanio ponders over the caskets, Portia's musicians urge him to use the inward eye of imagination in order to penetrate the riddle of the caskets. Fancy, they sing, is fed through the eyes by outward appearances, so let fancy die and allow the imagination of the higher world of mind to operate:

> Tell me where is fancy bred,
> Or in the heart or in the head?
> How begot, how nourished?
> Reply, reply.
> It is engend'red in the eyes,
> With gazing fed; and fancy dies
> In the cradle where it lies:
> Let us all ring fancy's knell,
> I'll begin it. Ding, dong, bell.

> 3.2.63–71

Bassanio takes the warning and ignores any fancy he might feel for the outward appearance of the caskets. With the inward eye of the imagination, he rejects the material beauty of the gold and silver and discovers the true gold hidden within the leaden casket. He is helped in this by the fact that he has already discovered the inward beauty of Portia and she in turn helps him, with this song, towards the union of their souls in marriage. The attractions of outward appearance that lead to love of the wrong woman, the love that Romeo felt for Rosaline, are due to fancy. True love demands the rare vision of the imagination and the inspiration to pursue that love.

While fancy or fantasy, rooted in earthly desire, is very often of the pleasant or sensual day-dream variety, it may also produce foolish or harmful images that can eventually run riot in a fevered mind. In *Henry IV Part 2*, it is related how Hotspur, with a too-small army and the fantastical belief that reinforcements were at hand, was suffering from this type of madness when he recklessly led his soldiers into battle:

> . . . [he] lined himself with hope,
> Eating the air and promise of supply,
> Flattering himself in project of a power
> Much smaller than the smallest of his thoughts,
> And so, with great imagination
> Proper to madmen, led his powers to death,
> And winking leaped into destruction.
>
> *Henry IV Part 2*, 1.3.27–33

Hotspur's madness arises from a seething brain that shapes fantasies and his behaviour is lunatic, as Theseus describes, but it is not the same frenzy that links poet and lover. This madness is divinely inspired and, while it may be called lunacy by those who have never experienced it for themselves, it is far removed from those who, caught within the dark aspect of the lunar goddess, see 'more devils than vast hell can hold'.

Macbeth is possessed of an imagination as great in its capacity for evil as his potential for nobility. As soon as he realises the witches' prophecy could come true, it gets to work, at first on the lower level of fantasy:

> Present fears
> Are less than horrible imaginings.
> My thought, whose murther yet is but fantastical,

Shakes so my single state of man,
That function is smother'd in surmise
And nothing is, but what is not.

1.3.137–42

His imagination is then reinforced by Lady Macbeth's own fantasies until his thoughts body forth into the physical reality of Duncan's murder. As he wrestles with his conscience before the murder, his imagination produces the unmanifest form of a dagger. He asks himself if this 'fatal vision' is a true product of his imagination or whether it is a dagger of the fanciful mind, a 'false creation', as it hovers over his choice between heaven and hell:

Is this a dagger, which I see before me,
The handle towards my hand? Come, let me clutch thee:
I have thee not, and yet I see thee still.
Art thou not, fatal vision, sensible
To feeling, as to sight? Or art thou but
A dagger of the mind, a false creation,
Proceeding from the heat-oppressed brain?

2.1.33–9

As with Macbeth, the imaginations of all Shakespeare's tragic heroes are well developed. They are all of noble minds who have had glimpses of reality before their imagination is clouded by the shadows of the physical world and they become a prey to the desires and emotions of the senses. Iago feeds Othello's strong imagination and, by sowing the seeds of the fanciful delusion that his wife has betrayed him, he throws Othello into the madness of jealousy. Cunningly, Iago suggests to Othello that even the noblest heart may entertain suspicious thoughts:

. . . who has a breast so pure,
But some uncleanly apprehensions
Keep leets and law-days, and in session sit
With meditations lawful?

3.3.141–4

Plotinus wrote of those men who pass their whole lives entirely in the world of sense objects while others desire a greater beauty and reality than that perceived through the senses but, unable to see what is above, descend again to the rational world.

> Others have risen a little from the things below because the better part of their soul has urged them on from the pleasant to a greater beauty; but since they were unable to see what is above, as they have no other ground to stand on they are brought down, with the name of virtue, to practical actions and choices of the things below from which they tried to raise themselves at first.[7]

With his deep desire for truth, Hamlet's imagination is stirred by the visitation of his father's ghost and, as he follows the apparition to 'a more remov'd ground', Horatio observes that 'he waxes desperate with imagination' (1.4.87). Instead of staying with the vision of beauty that he had seen in Ophelia, which would lead him to higher worlds, he descends to the rational world to struggle with the dilemma of whether he should really trust what he sees and hears and then whether he should perform the requested act of revenge. The Ghost presents a glimpse of hell rather than heaven, and Hamlet's rational mind is left to vie with his imagination over a problem that lies beyond the corporeal world of the senses. Therefore it is not surprising that seeing, in Theseus' words, 'more devils than vast hell can hold', his 'noble mind is o'erthrown' (3.1.152). But he also makes the positive choice of assuming a false madness by putting on, as he says, an antic disposition. This suggests an attempt to become possessed by a third type of divine madness which, as Plato describes, may be invoked to purge ancient blood-guilt:

> Again, where plagues and mightiest woes have bred in certain families, owing to some ancient blood-guiltiness, there madness has entered with holy prayers and rites, and by inspired utterances found a way of deliverance for those who are in need; and he who has part in this gift, and is truly possessed and duly out of his mind, is by the use of purifications and mysteries made whole and exempt from evil, future as well as present, and has a release from the calamity which was afflicting him.[8]

By this positive decision, Hamlet is attempting to deliver himself from ancient blood-guilt and thus exonerate the need to avenge his father's murder while, at the same time, allowing his hellish lunacy to be transformed into a divine madness.

However, in the end it is Ophelia, not Hamlet, whom 'madness has entered with holy prayers and rites': in her last scene she seems possessed by a divine frenzy as she attempts to find a way of deliverance through the ritual offering of flowers to her horrified family and friends.

These then are some of the seething fantasies that, if the path of love is abandoned for the tangled world of emotions and desires, may lead to tragedy and the lunacy of despair. But in Shakespeare's comedies, fantasy has the opportunity to be transformed into true imagination. Theseus may believe that the lovers' account of their experience in the Athenian wood is less than true, but Hippolyta understands that the lovers' dream is more than fancy's images: it is a transfiguring experience on their path of love that leads to something of great constancy. In this she is speaking of constancy as an archetypal form, a quality of the angelic mind:

> But all the story of the night told over,
> And all their minds transfigur'd so together,
> More witnesseth than fancy's images,
> And grows to something of great constancy;
> But howsoever, strange and admirable.
>
> 5.1.23–7

In *Antony and Cleopatra*, Cleopatra also has a dream, although its substance is of a higher order than the lovers' dream in the fairy wood. Describing a vision she has had of Antony as the ideal man, Cleopatra reveals an imagination fired with poetic frenzy:

> I dreamt there was an emperor Antony.
> O, such another sleep, that I might see
> But such another man! . . .
> His face was as the heavens, and therein stuck
> A sun and moon which kept their course and lighted
> The little O, the earth.
>
> 5.2.75–80

This is a vision of the imagination that releases Antony into the world of the gods and will be discussed in greater detail in Chapter 9.

On the other hand, in *Coriolanus* Shakespeare shows the limitations
of an image when it arises from fancy rather than imagination. The
overwhelming desire for a warrior son, with all the heroic virtues of
a soldier, produces a fanciful image of Coriolanus in the mind of his
mother, the Roman matriach Volumnia. As she herself says when wel-
coming him after a great victory, the idealised picture of him that she
has created from the buildings of her fancy has been realised:

> I have liv'd
> To see inherited my very wishes,
> And the building of my fancy: only
> There's one thing wanting . . .
>
> 2.1.196–9

The one thing that he lacks is not his election as consul, to which his
mother is referring, but love. Compare the loving image in Cleopatra's
imagination with the fanciful picture of Coriolanus in battle that
Volumnia gives her daughter-in-law:

> Methinks I hear hither your husband's drum;
> See him pluck Aufidius down by th'hair,
> As children from a bear, the Volsces shunning him.
> Methinks I see him stamp thus, and call thus:
> 'Come on you cowards, you were got in fear
> Though you were born in Rome.' His bloody brow
> With his mail'd hand then wiping, forth he goes
> Like to a harvest man that's task'd to mow
> Of all, or lose his hire.
>
> 1.3.29–37

She has not used her imagination to see the true picture of her son
balanced between warrior and lover, as Cleopatra imagined Antony,
but instead has painted half the image with fancy, conjured up in the
lower realm of the mind from sensory impressions. This lower mind,
ruled by reason, lacks true imagination and the ability to appreciate
the full dimension of the man so, while seeing the soldier, Volumnia
fails to see the lover. While Coriolanus has the courage of Mars, he
lacks the loving nature bestowed by Venus. He is handicapped by his
mother's incomplete vision and therefore, although he reaches the

heroic heights she fancied, he lacks the love to keep him there and he falls again to earth.

In a speech similar to Hippolyta's, Cleopatra explains the difference between the substance of imagination and fancy:

> But if there be nor ever were one such,
> It's past the size of dreaming. Nature wants stuff
> To vie strange forms with fancy; yet t'imagine
> An Antony were nature's piece 'gainst fancy,
> Condemning shadows quite.
>
> 5.2.95–9

Her picture of Antony is not fancy, she says, for nature can only create forms from ideas that lie in the real world of the imagination and it lacks the material to build such strange forms from mere fantasy. But the form that Cleopatra has seen in her imagination is a 'piece' or 'masterpiece' of nature. Antony appears as a god might, who takes on a human form and, because this form is in the imagination, it is against fancy and more real than the shadows of nature's forms that we perceive through our senses.

In the same passage in the *Phaedrus* on divine frenzy that was quoted earlier, Plato speaks of prophecy as another form of madness; thus, in *Richard II*, John of Gaunt on his death-bed prophesies with divine inspiration what will become of England, 'This royal throne of kings' (2.1.40):

> Methinks I am a prophet new inspired
> And thus expiring do foretell of him.
>
> 2.1.31–2

While ideas lie in the angelic world of the imagination, they all arise from the one source in God. It is He, the culmination of all the muses, who gives invention light, and is here addressed by Shakespeare in this sonnet as the tenth muse:

> How can my Muse want subject to invent,
> While thou dost breathe, that pour'st into my verse
> Thine own sweet argument, too excellent
> For every vulgar paper to rehearse?
> O, give thyself the thanks, if aught in me

Worthy perusal stand against thy sight,
For who's so dumb that cannot write to thee,
When thou thyself dost give invention light?
Be thou the tenth muse, ten times more in worth
Than those old nine which rhymers invocate,
And he that calls on thee, let him bring forth
Eternal numbers to outlive long date.
If my slight Muse do please these curious days,
The pain be mine, but thine shall be the praise.

Sonnet 38

On one level Shakespeare is addressing his beloved in human form, but on another he is speaking to God as divine beauty, for the fire of the creative imagination is the same bird-bolt of Berowne's that first awakens man's love. Transcending the brightest heaven of the angelic mind, it returns to its source in itself, the true Promethean fire or the one divine light of God. This is the moment that Shakespeare describes in *The Phoenix and the Turtle*, when the love of the turtle-dove burns in mutual flame with the fire of the phoenix and there is no distinction between them:

So between them love did shine
That the Turtle saw his right
Flaming in the Phoenix' sight
Either was the other's mine.

33–6

CHAPTER SEVEN

Something of Great Constancy

The One itself is above stability or motion, the
Angel is in stability, the Soul is equally in stability and in motion, and the Body is only in
motion.[1]

———•◦•———

I N THE LAST chapter, we looked at a speech by Theseus that showed
his confusion between imagination and fancy. Hippolyta's reply
showed that she understood how the lovers' story of their experiences in the wood was not a trick of fancy, but true imagination arising
from images in the angelic mind, the 'Angel' as Ficino calls it in the
quotation at the head of this chapter. This experience, she said, will
grow to 'something of great constancy', through which their souls may
attain the stability of their higher nature, the unchanging quality of the
heavenly world.

The soul is divided equally between stability and motion, and the
lover wins his beloved at the central point where its moving earthly part
meets its higher form in stability. Therefore, until his love is consolidated at the heavenly level, there remains the possibility that the heart
could fall from its relatively stable condition and become unfaithful. In
order for a permanent union to take place between the heavenly and
earthly worlds, a unity symbolised by the consummation of the marriage, the lover's constancy must be tested. If he is proved to be true,
the soul will have moved from motion to stability, from the earthly
world to the heavenly.

Constancy, therefore, is the quality of the unmoving world of the
angelic mind. When the soul becomes one with this world it reaches
an unmoving state and is constant to itself. In this sonnet, addressed
to the constant heart, Shakespeare is speaking of the divine state of his

own soul that is in love with the divine beauty of God, the prototype of all earthly beauty that will never fade.

> What is your substance, whereof are you made,
> That millions of strange shadows on you tend?
> Since every one hath, every one, one shade,
> And you, but one, can every shadow lend:
> Describe Adonis, and the counterfeit
> Is poorly imitated after you;
> On Helen's cheek all art of beauty set,
> And you in Grecian tires are painted new.
> Speak of the spring and foison of the year,
> The one doth shadow of your beauty show,
> The other as your bounty doth appear;
> And you in every blessèd shape we know.
> In all external grace you have some part,
> But you like none, none you, for constant heart.
>
> Sonnet 53

Substance means understanding or standing under[2] and is to the divine world what matter is to the material world. For instance, the matter of a sonnet consists of its vocabulary, metre, rhyme, imagery etc, but its substance is what, if any, understanding it conveys of the divine world to the higher mind. So here Shakespeare is exploring the substance of constancy by comparing the moving world with what is unmoving and at the same time he is conveying understanding of this truth to the angelic mind.

One of Shakespeare's most constant lovers is Silvius in *As You Like It*. His love is severely tested by Phoebe, the shepherdess whose dark eyes flash with Promethean fire, but not for love of him. He sacrifices all manly pride to prove his constancy in love, and is prepared to accept the man who reaps the 'main harvest' of her love if he can earn but a 'scatter'd smile':

> So holy and so perfect is my love,
> And I in such a poverty of grace,
> That I shall think it a most plenteous crop
> To glean the broken ears after the man
> That the main harvest reaps. Loose now and then
> A scatter'd smile, and that I'll live upon.
>
> 3.5.99–104

Because he remains constant and his love is 'so holy and so perfect', Silvius is at last allowed to win union with his soul. Having promised to marry Silvius if she refuses Ganymede, Phoebe is obliged to comply when the young shepherd lad turns out to be Rosalind, the disguised love of Orlando. His faith now catches her fancy, a declaration that, if indeed based on fancy alone, promises little for her constancy in the future!

> now thou art mine,
> Thy faith my fancy to thee doth combine.
>
> 5.4.148–9

In the same play, constancy is one of the lessons that Rosalind has been teaching her lover, Orlando. Acting as his tutor in the disguise of a shepherd boy, she bids him return for his next lesson at the appointed time. Although her tone is humorous, her message is deeply serious:

> ... if you break one jot of your promise, or come one minute behind your hour, I will think you the most pathetical break-promise, and the most hollow lover, and the most unworthy of her you call Rosalind, that may be chosen out of the gross band of the unfaithful; therefore beware my censure and keep your promise.
>
> 4.1.180–6

Proteus and Valentine, the two gentlemen of Verona, epitomise the inconstancy of earthly love and the constancy of spirit in the higher world. As a saint, the original Valentine rightly belongs to the spiritual realm, while Proteus was a Greek sea-god noted for his quixotic nature and his ability to change his shape into all manner of forms. Thus Bacon associates him with matter, the substance of the material world.[3] Proteus, having sworn his love for Julia, travels to join his friend, Valentine, at the court of the Duke, whose daughter, Sylvia, he is wooing. Throughout the play, Valentine remains true to his love, whom he sees as a 'heavenly saint', but Proteus, in whose eyes Sylvia is but an 'earthly paragon' (2.4.140–2), speedily shifts his love from Julia to this lower form of love:

> Even as one heat another heat expels,
> Or as one nail by strength drives out another,

> So the remembrance of my former love
> Is by a newer object quite forgotten.
>
> 2.4.188–91

The images he uses here of heat and nail, with his new love as an object in his eyes, are not those of a lover bound on the path towards heavenly love. He sees only her external beauty, whereas Valentine recognises her as 'divine' or at least in angelic form:

> . . . if not divine,
> Yet let her be a principality,
> Sovereign to all the creatures on the earth.
>
> 2.4.146–8

However, although she was easily forgotten, Proteus' true soul-mate remains faithful to him. Julia, disguised as a boy in the manner of all true souls whose love is not yet recognised, follows him to the duke's court and her constancy wins him in the end:

> What is in Sylvia's face but I may spy
> More fresh in Julia's, with a constant eye?
>
> 5.4.113–14

At the end of *The Two Gentlemen of Verona*, Julia presents Proteus with two rings, the ring he had given her before he left and the ring he had asked her as his servant to give to Sylvia. The ring is a symbol of constancy, an unbroken circle that Proteus breaks. Shakespeare uses this device again in *The Merchant of Venice*. Bassanio has won Portia through the trial of the caskets. However, before they can be married he has to leave her to attend the trial of his friend and benefactor, Antonio, during which he himself is given a trial, a test of his constancy. Portia, disguised as the young lawyer Bellario, saves Antonio from Shylock's demand for a pound of his flesh and, as a reward, she asks Bassanio for his ring, the ring she had given him at their marriage. Bassanio is placed in a terrible predicament for he is torn between duty to the young doctor and loyalty to the woman he loves. Either way his honour is at stake for, if a ring is given away to any other, the unity that the ring symbolises is broken and the giver proves his inability to remain faithful.

For Bassanio's soul to be so completely at one that it is ready for the next step into the angelic world of the mind, it must remain true and constant to itself. Constancy means standing firm in mind, being steadfast and true; it is a quality of the higher mind whose only movement, says Ficino, is that of turning itself towards God. The soul, on the other hand, may be moved unless it has the steadying influence of the mind:

> If there is any stability in the cognition of the Soul, it is stable thanks
> to the Mind rather than the Soul.[4]

Without that steadying influence, Ficino continues, it may be swayed by sensation or reason, which is just what happens to Bassanio when Portia as Belario asks for his ring. Reason demands that he has a duty to reward his friend's saviour and, overcome by the emotion of gratitude, he is swayed by Belario's reasonable argument and hands over the ring.

Shakespeare's device of having Portia disguised as a young lawyer is yet another example of how he personifies the higher soul, hiding her beauty in boy's attire so that she can act as tutor to her lover. Next time Bassanio and Portia meet, they are back in the world of the soul at Belmont and Portia is again in her own clothes; symbolically the veil that had covered her heavenly beauty is once more lowered. However, as his tutor, she rebukes him for his empty finger, symbol of his inconstancy:

> Even so void is your false heart of truth.
> By heaven I will ne'er come to your bed
> Until I see the ring!

> 5.1.189–91

Although he was misguided in giving the ring away, it was with honourable intention and it had unwittingly been returned to the constant heart from whom it was first received. So Bassanio is forgiven and, after he has sworn oaths of constancy—'I never more will break an oath with thee' (5.1.248)—they go to bed and he becomes one with his whole soul in the unmoving heavenly world.

More often in the tragedies the constant heart of the hero or lover is not only represented by the woman he loves but also by a faithful friend or loyal servant who supports and advises, following like

a guardian angel even when love has been rejected. It is not until
their friend and master has fallen deep into the darkness of chaos that
they disappear from view. Even then they may make a last attempt at
rescue, although they are helpless if the desire of the soul to make its
return is not present. Hamlet's fellow student, Horatio, whom he has
brought back with him from university, is a loyal comrade in contrast
to the false hearts of Rosencrantz and Guildenstern. Throughout
the first half of the play he is at Hamlet's side to advise and is his
only confidante. He disappears from the action after the play scene
that confirms to Hamlet Claudius' guilt in his father's murder: now
Hamlet's thoughts turn murderous and the constant heart cannot
follow into this dark night of the soul. The false friends, however, at
once make themselves evident, for Rosencrantz and Guildernstern
enter shortly after Horatio's last line. In the scene that follows Hamlet
appears to be raving, both to them and to Polonius, who enters a little
later, although his replies are actually most sane and reveal his aware-
ness of their endeavours to manipulate him. He accuses the younger
men of trying to play upon him as on a recorder:

> You would play upon me, you would seem to know my stops, you
> would pluck out the heart of my mystery, you would sound me from
> my lowest note to the top of my compass; and there is much music,
> excellent voice, in this little organ, yet cannot you make it speak.

3.2.355–60

As Polonius tries to humour Hamlet's apparently wandering mind,
agreeing with the different images he sees in the clouds, 'like a camel
. . . a weasel . . . or like a whale', Hamlet is only too aware of the false
nature of those left around him, who stretch his highly strung nerves
as taut as a bow, to their limit, 'They fool me to the top of my bent'
(3.2.369–75).

He has determined to assume 'an antic disposition' (1.5.180) but, once
alone, his soul falls into the lunacy of hellish darkness and, as his heart
hardens, his speech becomes as murderous as Macbeth's:

> 'Tis now the very witching time of night,
> When churchyards yawn and hell itself breathes out
> Contagion to this world. Now I could drink hot blood,

And do such bitter business as the day
Would quake to look on.

2.379–83

The dark place into which he then enters will be discussed in Chapter 12, but it is notable that throughout the following scenes, before Hamlet leaves for England, Horatio is absent. However, the turning point of the soul has been reached and, after Hamlet's experiences at sea, with his capture by pirates and the discovery of Claudius' plan to have him killed in England, the first person he contacts by letter is his faithful friend and the constant heart to which he is now returning, Horatio. Horatio is there to greet Hamlet home and to witness his grief at Ophelia's death and his acknowledgement of the love he had rejected—'I lov'd Ophelia' (5.1.264). Once back at the court, he is on hand to warn him against fighting Laertes in what will become the fateful duel at the end of the play. Hamlet, however, accepts the challenge and his destiny as divine providence. As he dies, wounded by Laertes' poisoned sword, he lies cradled by Horatio as if indeed in the arms of his guardian angel. It is Horatio who recognises the recovery of Hamlet's nobility of heart and heralds his entry into the heavenly world with the beautiful lines:

Now cracks a noble heart. Good night, sweet prince,
And flights of angels sing thee to thy rest.

5.2.364–5

In *Timon of Athens,* the faithful servant is Timon's Steward, the keeper of his accounts and household affairs, who sees his master ruined by the false friends preying on his generous nature. His warnings fall on deaf ears and he is forced to watch his master's financial ruin and descent from philanthropy to hatred of his fellow men. Timon has a good and noble heart but, lacking discrimination, he has succumbed to the flattery of false suitors for his affection who seek only financial gain. His mind is beguiled by the outward shows of the material world—paintings, poems and jewels brought by artists and merchants—and the insincere friendship of those greedy for his money. Having been drained dry, he has to borrow so that his beneficence may continue. When financial ruin is imminent, his so-called friends fade away. His spiritual wealth has also been dissipated. The only good and true impulses that remain with him are his servants but, because of the waste of their master's fortune, they too are impoverished and have to disperse. Using the analogy of his house as Timon's soul, the Steward refers to its faithful servants as 'broken implements of a ruin'd house', to which one of them replies:

> Yet do our hearts bear Timon's livery,
> That see I by our faces; we are fellows still,
> Serving alike in sorrow. Leak'd is our bark,
> And we, poor mates, stand on the dying deck,
> Hearing the surges threat; we all must part
> Into this sea of air.
>
> 4.2.16–22

Like Prospero's spirits they depart into airy nothing, although first the Steward shares with them all that he has left. Such is the bounty of the constant heart.

Banishing his wretched, barren soul to the desert, Timon rails against humanity but, even in the extremity of hatred both of himself and all mankind, he is visited by the good Steward who goes out to find him and offers to continue his services at his own expense. The constant heart offers a divine spark of love and begs to be known, even when the soul has cast itself out into the darkness of despair:

> I beg of you to know me, good my lord
> T'accept my grief and while this poor wealth lasts
> To entertain me as your steward still.
>
> 4.3.491–3

There are a number of other servants who provide an ideal of constancy from which their masters may waver or fall but who always await their soul's return. The constant heart of Pisanio, the servant of Posthumus in *Cymbeline,* is left to guard Imogen, the higher part of his master's soul, during his absence. Believing Imogen to be unfaithful to him, Posthumus writes a letter to Pisanio asking him to kill his wife. However, unable to murder the soul, he hides her in the guise of a boy until such time as his master has found truth once more in his heart. Despite his jealousy and temporary inability to see that his soul, to whom he is united by marriage, could never be unfaithful, Pisanio continues to be true to Posthumus and believe in him:

> . . . to prove false, which I will never be,
> To him that is most true.
>
> 3.5.159–60

A faithful friend who becomes a servant is the Duke of Kent in *King Lear*. Kent has been banished by the king for daring to protest at his rejection of Cordelia, but he returns in disguise so that he may continue to serve his friend. Heavenly love, such as Cordelia represents, cannot enter such depths as those into which Lear has plunged, even in disguise, but the constant heart in its male form may disguise itself like Kent and care for his master still. Kent speaks to himself of his resolution to remain with Lear:

> Now banish'd Kent,
> If thou canst serve where thou dost stand condemn'd,
> So may it come, thy master, whom thou lov'st,
> Shall find thee full of labours.
>
> 1.4.4–7

Despite being put in the stocks for defending his master, Kent remains at Lear's side and brings him through his ordeal. At the end of the play, after Lear's death, he is offered joint leadership of the country but refuses it. His answer appears ambiguous, but what he has always seen in his master, and to which he has remained constant, is divine kingship. Having served an earthly king with such devotion, he now goes to join God, the divine ruler:

> I have a journey, sir, shortly to go;
> My master calls me, I must not say no.
>
> 5.3.320–1

The faithful friend or servant is not found as frequently in the comedies, but one of the most devoted servants—because his age and health are beyond the physical effort required for the final service he has to offer—is old Adam in *As You Like It*. His devotion might have earned him a place in one of the great tragedies, but his duty in this comedy is to accompany his young master on his first steps on the path of love. Formerly the servant of Orlando's father, his faithful service continues with the son and he insists that he accompany him into the forest of Arden, where he is escaping from his jealous brother's anger.

He offers him his life savings and vows he can still 'do the service of a younger man' (2.3.54). Orlando praises his constancy and the service that is offered from duty and not for financial gain:

> O good old man, how well in thee appears
> The constant service of the antique world,
> When service sweat for duty, not for need.
>
> 2.3.56–8

Adam's duty takes him to the forest but his strength is spent in the effort. He has, however, set Orlando on his way and, because he finally collapses, Orlando seeks help at the encampment of the banished Duke. It is left for Rosalind to teach Orlando all the constancy that he needs as a lover, but the unmoving love of the old retainer will surely ring in his ears all his life:

> Master go on, and I will follow thee
> To the last gasp with truth and loyalty.
>
> 2.3.69–70

CHAPTER EIGHT

Unshak'd of Motion

Yet in the number I do know but one
That unassailable holds on his rank,
Unshak'd of motion; and that I am he.

Julius Caesar 3.1.68–70

———•·•———

FICINO EXPLAINS each of the Platonic worlds as having a particular movement in relation to time and space, describing them as four concentric circles. God is the single, unmoving centre and, while this point is beyond form, space or time, the outer circle of the body is subject to all of these. It has a multiplicity of forms and is controlled by time and limited by space and the movement of other bodies. Nearest to God, the angelic mind contains the many forms of archetypal ideas and the seed forms of the imagination but, with regard to movement, it remains constant and still. Like Venus, the soul has something of both body and mind, of heaven and earth. As with the Inigo Jones model, it lies between both worlds, the upper soul belonging to the unmoving airy heavens and the lower to the restless watery earth. While the soul has 'multiplicity of parts and passions, and is subject to change, both in the process of thinking and in fluctuations of mood',[1] it is not, like the body, limited to space, and its movement may be stabilised by the higher mind.

The movements of the worlds, in both their universal and personal senses, are integral to *Julius Caesar*. Brutus calls 'the state of man, / Like to a little kingdom' (2.1.67–8) and, as the Roman leader, Julius Caesar is a representation of Rome itself. When Antony speaks of 'the three-fold world divided' (4.1.14), he is referring not only to the Roman world split into the three parts of the triumvirate formed after Caesar's death, but also to the three Platonic worlds.

79

Writing on the duty of a citizen, Ficino calls attention to the single being of the state of which its citizens are a part:

> It is the duty of a citizen to consider the state as a single being formed of its citizens who are the parts; and that the parts should serve the whole, not the whole the parts.[2]

A similar concept is to be found in *Coriolanus,* where Menenius describes the citizens of Rome as not serving the whole body but rebelling against the 'belly' of the state:

> The senators of Rome are this good belly,
> And you the multitudinous members . . .
>
> 1.1.147–8

At the opening of *Julius Caesar,* Caesar has the support of the working people, the body of Rome. They wish to 'make holiday to see Caesar, and rejoice in his triumph' (1.1.30–1) over the sons of Pompey. But, as Ficino tells us, the body is the most easily moved of all the worlds: the Tribunes have little trouble in deflecting their celebrations and sending them back to work. Their rapid movement in allegiance is even more dramatic when, having been convinced by Brutus that the murder of Caesar has been for their good and for the good of Rome, they are swiftly moved to mutiny by Antony's inspired oratory.

Caesar himself is described by Antony as 'the noblest man' (3.1.256) and although he is speaking from envy even Cassius calls him 'a god who doth stride the narrow world like a Colossus' (1.2.133–4). These are both descriptions worthy of Cleopatra's eulogy on Antony in the later play, in which she envisions the full potential of Antony as an enlightened man, a god in the angelic world. Apart from Brutus, all the conspirators envy Caesar, although their envy is expressed as a fear of his ambitions. Because the parts do not serve the whole, the body of Rome causes its own disruption as well as Caesar's downfall. Caesar's vulnerability to these emotions is reflected in his physical body by the falling sickness, the antithesis to the rising ambition of which he is accused. This explains the observation made by Cassius that so puzzles Casca:

> No, Caesar hath it not; but you, and I,
> And honest Casca, we have the falling sickness.
>
> 1.2.252–3

It is also significant that Caesar and his wife, Calpurnia, are childless. As a child represents the consummation of a physical marriage, so, Ficino says, the flowering of a spiritual union is also a child:

> Just as the human body is pregnant. . . so the soul is pregnant, and both are stimulated to childbearing by the incitements of love.[3]

The spiritual child of the soul is the enlightened man. His spirit embraces the higher world of the Angelic Mind, from whence there is only one more step to be taken into complete unity with God. Thus it is interesting that the first person whom Caesar addresses in the play is his wife, Calpurnia: he urges her to cure herself of barrenness by standing in the path of Antony, who is participating in a ritual race. To be touched by a runner in such a race would cure a woman, it was believed, of the 'sterile curse' (1.2.9). Antony is a man who is ruled by love and in this play he represents the power of love: it is only he who truly loves Caesar and he sways the populace by persuading them of Caesar's love both for Brutus and for them. Thus the power of his touch as a runner could produce not only a child of the body, as the superstition ran, but also a spiritual growth of the soul through love. Without love, both Caesar and Rome are prevented from entering fully into the heavenly world.

Although Caesar has one foot, so to speak, in the higher world, because he lacks absolute love of the divine his position is not yet stabilised. Still in the shaky world of the unstable soul, Caesar reaches for the stars in an attempt to exchange both his own and Rome's precarious positions for the heavenly world. It is for this reason that he devotes a whole speech to constancy:

> But I am constant as the northern star,
> Of whose true-fix'd and resting quality
> There is no fellow in the firmament.
> The skies are painted with unnumber'd sparks,
> They are all fire, and every one doth shine;
> But there's but one in all doth hold his place.
> So in the world: 'tis furnish'd well with men,

> And men are flesh and blood, and apprehensive;
> Yet in the number I do know but one
> That unassailable holds on his rank,
> Unshak'd of motion; and that I am he.
>
> 3.1.60–70

In the imagination, the angelic form is created as an image in the material world, so Caesar, speaking these words, takes on the role of divine kingship, the unassailable One whom he represents on earth, constant and unshak'd of motion. Above all the worlds, 'the One remains above number, motion and place'[4] and Caesar, in the last three lines of the above speech, clearly states his position as that One.

Now whether Caesar can come near to fulfilling the role he sees so clearly in his imagination is another matter. But in one sense, although he may in fact lack the stability that he is so eager to profess, he is speaking the absolute truth, for man *is* divine: 'Ye are gods',[5] Ficino instructs his students. On the other hand, although Caesar has reached the point of acknowledging his divinity, his soul has not yet brought forth the fruits of love. Without this stability of the soul, he is as open to envy as the body of Rome is open to rapid emotional change.

The wife of Brutus, Portia, is the one truly constant character in *Julius Caesar*. The patient sufferance of her self-inflicted wound in the thigh is proof of the constancy both of the soul of her husband and of her own mind. She will never disclose her husband's secrets:

> I have made strong proof of my constancy,
> Giving myself a voluntary wound
> Here, in the thigh.
>
> 2.1.299–301

Such constancy commands the respect of her husband who recognises it as one of the virtues of the angelic mind:

> O ye gods,
> Render me worthy of this noble wife!
>
> 2.1.302–3

She is not alone in her constancy and nobility of mind since there are many references to the same qualities in Brutus. As a married couple, they are one in body and soul, but they have travelled further along the path than most, for their virtues indicate both Brutus and Portia have knowledge of the higher world. Therefore she has no option but to remain true to her husband, even though her own heart, in compassion and mercy for Caesar, is calling on her to inform against the conspirators. She begs constancy itself, as if it were a living being, to come to her aid:

> O constancy, be strong upon my side;
> Set a huge mountain 'tween my heart and tongue
>
> 2.4.6–7

On the other hand, the soul of Brutus is speaking through his conscience, which tells him that if his love for Caesar is true he could not be his assassin. Love is the prime mover of the universe that should never be sacrificed at any cost, but it is Antony who acts truly from love, while Brutus believes that his actions are for the good of the state. Instead of remaining constant to love, Brutus has been persuaded to join the conspiracy against Caesar by the reasonable argument of Cassius. In other words, instead of following his noble mind, he has become susceptible to reason that has command over the moving physical world. Cassius is well aware of this:

> Well, Brutus, thou art noble; yet I see
> Thy honourable mettle may be wrought
> From that it is dispos'd: therefore 'tis meet
> That noble minds keep ever with their likes;
> For who so firm that cannot be seduc'd?
>
> 1.2.305–9

The mutual love and respect between Brutus and Cassius is stressed. In one respect, their friendship unites them as one being, with Cassius reflecting the dark side of Brutus's nature and, at the same time, the dark side of the universe. At the start of his reasoned argument in favour of the assassination, Cassius tells Brutus:

> And since you know you cannot see yourself
> So well as by reflection, I, your glass,
> Will modestly discover to yourself
> That of yourself which you yet know not of.
>
> 1.2.66–9

Brutus, swayed by Cassius into becoming part of the conspiracy to murder Caesar, is allowing his nature to fall into darkness; this is the darkness of chaos, the unformed matter from which all worlds arise. So, when Caesar is murdered, the bonds that have held the worlds of Rome and Brutus in equable balance are broken and the forces of darkness are freed. Almost before Brutus has made up his mind to join the conspirators, the gods, who in these situations act as the powers of nature, display their anger in a series of unnatural events in the physical world. A passage was quoted in Chapter 3 in which Casca arrives breathlessly on the scene to report that the strange happenings on the streets are far beyond the laws of nature, and that the gods, incensed by the behaviour of the world, have sent tempests and earthquakes for its destruction.

As the physical world is a reflection of the heavenly, it should ideally reflect the harmony of the higher. Therefore, any agitation that arises in the volatile world of human nature and emotions needs to be tempered or balanced in the soul through the power of love. This tempering may require some upheaval and so, before harmony can be restored in the state of Rome after Caesar's murder, the strife of war is necessary if the balance of nature is to be rectified; in love and war Venus and Mars are forever entwined. The readjustment begins with Mark Antony's funeral oration, during which he enlists the power of love to incite the crowd into action against the conspirators, who in turn take up arms in civil war.

The rest of the play is not so much about Caesar's revenge, as critics often claim, but the realignment of the natures of Rome and her leaders through the vicissitudes of war so that heaven may once again be in harmony with earth. The final symbolic act that brings this about is the death of Brutus by his own hand. His entry into the dark side of his nature has been brief and his quarrel with Cassius signifies his return to honesty and nobility. By refusing to budge from his declaration that Cassius was wrong to condone the taking of bribes, he reveals once more the constancy of his soul and in their reconciliation, as Cassius offers his 'hand' and Brutus his 'heart' (4.3.116–17), his physical nature is reconciled with his loving soul. However, his part in the renaissance of Rome requires the final sacrifice, for there can be no rebirth without death. At their reconciliation, Brutus tells Cassius the strange tale of how his wife died by her own hand. Fearing that the war was going against Brutus, she 'swallow'd fire' (4.3.155). The incident is taken from Plutarch but it would be fitting for the higher Soul to consume the Promethean fire of love and die so that Rome may be reborn. Expiring in a blaze of divine light, the human soul is drawn towards heaven in an act of true constancy. Once the soul has died a physical death, both Brutus and his mirror image, Cassius, also die of their own volition.

In their death, the spiritual marriage of Brutus and Portia now flowers into a new golden age for Rome. Shakespeare often gives the last words of a play to the symbolic child of spiritual rebirth and here it is Caesar's adopted son, Octavius Caesar, who inherits the reunified Rome. However, before Octavius speaks the closing lines, Antony, representing the power of love, applauds the life of Brutus. All the elements of his virtues having been tempered according to the divine image, his death now brings the moveable worlds into harmony with the constant world of the angelic mind:

> His life was gentle, and the elements
> So mix'd in him, that Nature might stand up
> And say to all the world, 'This was a man!'
>
> 5.5.73–5

CHAPTER NINE

Venus and Mars

———•◦•———

T HE THEME of constancy continues in *Antony and Cleopatra*, but in this play it enters the realm of the gods, the world of higher mind that Caesar desired but was unable to attain. While most of Shakespeare's young lovers are setting out on the first stages of the path of love, the mature lovers in *Antony and Cleopatra* have consummated their love in the soul, which now teeters between the earthly and heavenly worlds. The emotional play of the moving physical world is contrasted with the stillness of the constant heart. Their story, however, may be seen not only at the human level but also at the universal. As lovers, they have been drawn by each other's beauty to become united in the world of the soul. Antony is from Rome, a material world of action ruled by reason; he is a leader of this world, a courageous soldier whose soul is drawn by love to its heavenly part that lies with Cleopatra in Egypt. Shakespeare follows their path of love in five stages, which more or less correspond with the five acts, although it should be remembered that Shakespeare wrote the play without act divisions. At the start their love idles in physical voluptuousness, then reason takes over and Antony breaks away to Rome. Love calls him back to his soul in Egypt, where reason and love engage in battle before reuniting in harmony. Love is again put to the test and, in apparent failure, he undergoes the death of the body. But love is merciful; in death he is reunited with his beloved and reborn through the world of the imagination as universal man.

Within the first lines of the play, Philo, whose name denotes a loving friend, reveals his insight into higher worlds by referring to Antony as 'the triple pillar of the world' (1.1.12). This is not only because he is a member of the ruling triumvirate of Rome but also because, as a man

Botticelli, Venus and Mars, *National Gallery, London*

of great stature, he is seen to contain the attributes of all three worlds. But there is no harmony between these worlds: reason is at odds with the pleasures of love. At ease in Egypt, Antony prefers the company of Cleopatra to entertaining the messengers from Rome. Philo again comments:

> . . . when he is not Antony,
> He comes too short of that great property
> Which still should go with Antony.
>
> 1.1.58–60

Torn between physical love and reason, it is only by understanding and dwelling in the higher parts of his soul and mind that he can find peace. Captivated by Cleopatra, he has become a 'strumpet's fool' (1.1.13). In order to become his true self, his 'great property', as Philo calls it, Antony must learn to stand on his own. He should be supported by love but not dominated by it. At their first entry together, Cleopatra asks Antony to set a limit on their love, to which he replies, 'thou needs find out new heaven, new earth' (1.1.17). The limit can only be the source of love which is God and, to find God, they must seek out the angelic world of universal mind.

While Antony and Cleopatra together follow the path of love as human souls, they also represent archetypes of the heavenly world. In the angelic mind, all the ideas of the Creator's imagination are held like the seeds of every possible form of creation. So at this level, Antony and Cleopatra may be understood as those archetypal seed forms that contain all the potential of courage and the power of love. These archetypes are the gods, known by their Roman names and still familiar to us today in their planetary forms. Ficino's astrology, that became popularised in Renaissance England through *De harmonia mundi*, written in 1525 by the Venetian friar Francesco Giorgi and substantiated later by Robert Fludd, places the sun between Venus and Mars. Thus the soul lies in the position of transformer where she may bring Mars, the archetype of strife and war, into harmony with the beauty of love. In his painting of Venus and Mars, Botticelli, a master of harmonious composition who was strongly influenced by Ficino, shows how the goddess of love has gently overcome the god of war: sleeping after their union, he is so drowsy with the harmony that even the playful satyrs cannot wake him. Myth tells of a daughter, born to Venus and Mars, named Harmonia: she is harmony, the offspring of strife and love.

Thus, as courage and the power of love, Antony and Cleopatra play out their roles as Mars and Venus. At the human level, they are lovers, but in the divine world they are gods, whose function is to bring the heavenly and earthly worlds into balance and harmony. These roles are signified many times during the play: Antony as the figure of Mars is clearly established during Philo's opening lines:

> Nay, but this dotage of our general's
> O'erflows the measure: those his goodly eyes,
> That o'er the files and musters of the war
> Have glowed like plated Mars, now bend, now turn
> The office and devotion of their view
> Upon a tawny front.

1.1.1–6

Later, wondering 'what Venus did with Mars' (1.5.19), Mardian the eunuch turns our thoughts again towards the gods, while Enobarbus gives his immortal description of Cleopatra in her barge, a Venus beyond the imagination of any artist:

> For her own person,
> It beggared all description: she did lie
> In her pavilion, cloth-of-gold of tissue,
> O'er-picturing that Venus where we see
> The fancy outwork nature.

2.2.207–11

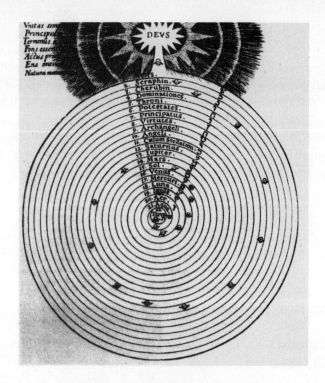

Diagram of the spheres by Robert Fludd,
Utriusque cosmi, *Oppenheim, 1617*

As a goddess she is immortal and her virtues eternal:

> Age cannot wither her, nor custom stale
> Her infinite variety.

> 2.2.245–6

Ficino describes the infinite variety of the heavenly Venus who guides the lover towards the divine world in a letter to Lorenzo de' Medici:

> For indeed, her soul and spirit are love and kinship; her eyes are majesty and magnanimity; her hands are liberality and greatness in action; her feet, gentleness and restraint. Finally, her whole is harmony and integrity, honour and radiance.[3]

These qualities balance and harmonise the virtues of Mars for, while Mars possesses courage and greatness of soul, he is prone to anger:

If Venus comes near, she does not impede that virtue of magnanimity given by Mars, but she does restrain the vice of irascibility. Here
she seems to make Mars more gentle and thus to dominate him.[2]

Whilst this is the heavenly aspect of Venus, it is clear that within
Cleopatra's infinite variety are the appetites of the lower Venus, whose
beauty attracts the lover towards sexual rather than divine love:

The heavenly Venus strives, through its intelligence, to reproduce in
itself as exactly as possible the beauty of the higher things; the vulgar
Venus strives, through the fertility of its divine seeds, to reproduce
in the Matter of the World the beauty which is divinely conceived
within itself.[3]

When the play opens, Cleopatra is too much the earthly Venus. By
holding Antony in physical love, she is impeding his magnanimity
and restricting his noble, courageous, high, unmatchable spirit (2.3.19).
Realising the danger, he breaks away:

> These strong Egyptian fetters I must break,
> Or lose myself in dotage
>
> 1.2.122–3

Although she still feels rejected, she does let him go with fairly good
grace in the end, realising that his honour, which pertains to his true
nature, is at stake:

> Your honour calls you hence
> Therefore be deaf to my unpitied folly,
> And all the gods go with you
>
> 1.3.99–101

Returning to Rome, Antony strengthens his alliance with Octavius
Caesar by marrying his sister. Although Octavia is a model of love's
temperance and gives him her whole-hearted support, she is not his
true soul-mate and he realises that, sooner or later, he must return
to Egypt. None other than Cleopatra, his Venus with the power of
heavenly love, can help him to fulfil his destiny. Besides, as the most
active and powerful member of the triumvirate with whom Antony
rules Rome, Octavius Caesar is also his rival. If a man is to reach his

true stature, he must have the space to expand and this space can be shared with no other. Antony is beginning to appreciate this when his own knowledge that Octavius is standing in his light speaks to him through the words of the soothsayer: 'Thy lustre thickens / When he shines by' (2.3.26–7). The growing unease between Antony and Caesar erupts into the anger of Mars and war is declared. While Octavia tries in vain to make peace between her husband and her brother, Antony returns to Cleopatra.

Cleopatra now has another chance to support Antony in his Martian exploits but, overcompensating for her previous restrictions, she decides to join in the battle herself and, forsaking her role of Venus, she attempts the work of Mars. Antony also overcompensates for his previous idleness and acts with unreasonable bravura. He allows valour to prey on his reason and decides to fight a sea-battle for the only reason that Caesar dares them to it. On the practical level, Antony's army is better suited to fighting on the land, being 'war-mark'd footmen' (3.7.44) rather than mariners, but, in the world of the gods, water is not a suitable element for Mars. Water belongs to the emotions and Mars needs to be firmly grounded in earth; even air or fire, as Antony later admits (4.10.3), would be preferable to water. With Antony out of his element and Cleopatra in the wrong role, the consequences are dire. Cleopatra, caught in the midst of the battle at sea, succumbs to its emotional whirlpool and flees in terror; Antony, having lost his reason and being caught entirely by his emotions, has no option but to follow his heart:

> Egypt, thou knewst too well,
> My heart was to thy rudder tied by th' strings
> And thou shouldst tow me after. O'er my spirit
> Thy full supremacy thou knewst, and that
> Thy beck might from the bidding of the gods
> Command me.

3.11.56–61

Later, furious at Cleopatra's surrender to Caesar, Antony can see her only as the earthly Venus. He berates her for lacking the virtue of temperance belonging to her heavenly counterpart:

I found you as a morsel, cold upon
Dead Caesar's trencher; nay, you were a fragment
Of Gnaeus Pompey's, besides what hotter hours,
Unregister'd in vulgar fame, you have
Luxuriously pick'd out. For I am sure
Though you can guess what temperance should be,
You know not what it is

3.13.121–7

Her spirited avowal of her love, however, unites them once more in loving harmony, while Antony swears that henceforth his valour will know no bounds. Balanced between love and reason, Cleopatra declares that 'since my lord / Is Antony again, I will be Cleopatra' (3.13.191–2). With Venus and Mars once more in balance and fulfilling their rightful roles, harmony is reborn.

Acting with the magnanimity and gentleness of Mars, Antony asks his servants to be sure that, on the eve of the battle, the meal they will be serving to his household is a bounteous one. His generosity continues with his forgiveness of Enobarbus for his desertion; Enobarbus in gratitude calls him a 'mine of bounty' (4.6.33). After his death, bounty is one of the universal qualities that Cleopatra extols in Antony—'his bounty, / There was no winter in't' (5.2.85–6)—for generosity of spirit is part of the greatness of soul that Ficino connects with Mars.

Cleopatra now gives Antony her full support and, as she helps him to prepare for battle, assisted by his servant Eros, the image is that of the heavenly Venus buckling on the armour of Mars. Now that both are performing in their proper spheres, the day is won and Antony returns in triumph. Having escaped the snares of the world, the chains of love no longer restrict and, addressing each other in the exalted language of the gods, the pair are drawn together as one:

ANTONY: O thou day o'th' world,
    Chain mine armed neck! Leap thou, attire and all,
    Through proof of harness to my heart—
CLEOPATRA: Lord of lords!
    O infinite virtue. Com'st thou smiling from
    The world's great snare uncaught?

4.8.13–18

Now that the heavenly virtues are balanced in the physical world and the soul is in harmony, Antony calls for the earthly music that will sound in accord with the music of heaven:

> Trumpeters,
> With brazen din blast you the city's ear,
> Make mingle with our rattling tambourines,
> That heaven and earth may strike their sounds together.
>
> 4.8.35–8

It is at this point that Antony is put to his final test of faith in love, and fails. With the battle going against him, he believes that he has been betrayed by Cleopatra, whose soul he thought was his—'O this false soul of Egypt!' (4.12.25). Now his anger knows no bounds and Cleopatra, terrified, flees to the monument, hoping that if Antony believes she is dead his anger will turn to pity. Her plan succeeds to a far greater extent than she ever wished. Overcome with grief and remorse at the news of her apparent death, Antony determines to die himself. He asks for the help of his servant, Eros, who had earlier assisted Cleopatra with his armour. This servant is well named, for whereas Cleopatra represents Venus, the power of love, Eros is the name of love itself. So now love comes to Antony's aid, but not in the way he expects. As a loyal servant, Eros is unable to refuse his wishes but, rather than kill the master he loves, he turns the sword upon himself. By this act, the love of Eros has forced Antony into a position where he has to take his own life, thus ensuring that, according to Roman belief, he dies a noble death.

Before Antony falls onto his sword he describes his death as a marriage or, in the terms of the soul, a union:

> . . . I will be
> A bridegroom in my death and run into't
> As to a lover's bed.
>
> 4.14.100–2

It is necessary for his death to be delayed until he can be brought into final union with his soul, who awaits him in the tomb-like monument. Shakespeare is not asking for an unnecessary, and what is often an awkward, stage device as Cleopatra draws Antony up to the top

of the monument, he is offering a powerful visual symbol to his
audience. In his comedies, Shakespeare is fond of using the idea of the
lover being baited like a fish. For instance, in *Much Ado About Nothing*
Beatrice and Benedick are baited in turn by their friends who, making
certain that their conversations are overheard, trick them into believing
that each is loved by the other:

> The pleasant'st angling is to see the fish
> Cut with her golden oars the silver stream,
> And greedily devour the treacherous bait:
> So angle we for Beatrice.
>
> 3.1.26–9

Antony had long ago been baited in the first stages of love and is now
ready to be drawn up by Cleopatra to the heavenly world of the gods.
Ficino uses the same imagery:

> The soul, consumed by the divine brilliance which shines in the
> beauteous man as though in a mirror, is seized unknowingly by
> that brilliance, and is drawn upward as by a hook, so that the soul
> becomes God.[4]

In the light of this statement, it is now clear that Cleopatra is herself consumed by the divine brilliance which is mirrored in Antony
and, calling on the gods to aid her, she draws him up to die, not as a
mortal, but as one about to achieve immortality in the divine world:

> Had I great Juno's power,
> The strong-wing'd Mercury should fetch thee up,
> And set thee by Jove's side.
>
> 4.15.35–7

With the death of the physical body, his spirit is released and, after
burying him, there is nothing more for Cleopatra to do except to
follow:

> We'll bury him: and then, what's brave, what's noble,
> Let's do it in the high Roman fashion,
> And make death proud to take us. Come away,
> His case of that huge spirit now is cold.
>
> 4.15.90–3

Nobility, like constancy, is a god-like virtue and Cleopatra follows
Antony's example by dying a noble death at her own hand. She is
now fixed in the constant world of the angelic mind as the heavenly
Venus, utterly forsaking the earthly goddess ruled by the ever-changing
moon:

> Now from head to foot
> I am marble-constant. Now the fleeting moon
> No planet is of mine.
>
> 5.2.238–40

She has immortal longings to rejoin the man she can now call husband
in the world of fire and air, the new heaven where, as Antony had told
her at the beginning of the play, they would find the ultimate love.

> Husband, I come!
> Now to that name my courage prove my title!
> I am fire and air; my other elements
> I give to baser life.
>
> 5.2.286–9

As personifications of the gods, Antony and Cleopatra are Mars and
Venus, but as themselves they reach the perfect balance of all the virtues
of the gods, proving that men are, as Ficino said, divine:

Why have you been looking at the ground for so long, divine men?
Look up, citizens of the heavenly country, denizens of the earth.
Man is an earthly star enveloped in a cloud; but a star is a heavenly
man.[5]

Cleopatra prepares for her death as if she was already in the archetypal world of the gods and her vision is lit by the light of inspiration
in the angelic mind. She sees Antony in all his glory as the heavenly
man:

> I dreamt there was an emperor Antony.
> O, such another sleep, that I might see
> But such another man! . . .
> His face was as the heavens, and therein stuck
> A sun and moon, which kept their course, and lighted
> The little O, the earth. . . .

His legs bestrid the ocean; his rear'd arm
Crested the world: his voice was propertied
As all the tuned spheres, and that to friends:
But when he meant to quail, and shake the orb,
He was as rattling thunder. For his bounty,
There was no winter in't; an Antony it was
That grew the more by reaping. His delights
Were dolphin-like; they showed his back above
The element they lived in: in his livery
Walk'd crowns and crownets: realms and islands were
As plates dropp'd from his pocket.

5.2.75–91

Through Cleopatra's leap of the imagination into the divine world, both she and Antony fulfil their destiny. Man as the universe, universal man: herein lies the true dimension of Shakespeare's plays.

CHAPTER TEN

A Most Rare Vision

———•·•———

A S WITH ALL true visions of the imagination, Cleopatra's is of the heavenly world. Written within the scope of Shakespeare's own huge imagination, *A Midsummer Night's Dream* presents us with imagination and fancy, vision and dream, as the path of love unfolds. The play is framed by the physical world in which its inhabitants have all the potential for spiritual growth. Athens, ruled by Theseus, is the world of cause and effect, a moveable world ruled by the reasonable mind and the emotions. Theseus is a reasonable man but one who, as we know from his long speech on the imagination, has had inklings of other worlds. But it is Hippolyta who really understands these worlds—as she well might for, according to the myth, she was herself descended from the gods, her father being Mars, the god of war. Warlike herself, she became the queen of the Amazons and, like the goddess Diana, a huntress. It was she, it will be remembered, who corrected the attempt by Theseus to pass off the account of the lovers' midnight adventures in the wood as mere fantasy:

> But all the story of the night told over,
> And all their minds transfigur'd so together,
> More witnesseth than fancy's images,
> And grows to something of great constancy;
> But howsoever, strange and admirable.
>
> 5.1.23–7

The fact that all their minds have been transfigured together, and each of their stories supports the other, indicates that what the lovers went through during their night in the wood was indeed a real experience and not mere fancy. While the events of the night are strange and admirable, Hippolyta's reference to their great constancy shows

97

that they have taken place in the unmoving angelic mind, the world of true imagination beyond time and space. In this context the 'dream' of the title refers to something lying much closer to reality than the shadows of the physical forms we see whilst apparently 'awake' and habitually call the truth.

Framed by events in the material world at the court of Theseus, the world of the imagination in the wood is full of spirits, the forms of the imagination. They are the fairies whom Shakespeare introduces as soon as the scene changes from court to wood. The first fairy to appear is addressed by Puck as a spirit: 'How now, spirit? Whither wander you?' (2.1.1).

The moon plays an important role in the play and is used to differentiate the earthly from the spiritual world. It is mentioned during the opening words of the play, always a clue to understanding where Shakespeare intends to take his audience, thus stressing its significance:

> Now fair Hippolyta, our nuptial hour
> Draws on apace; four happy days bring in
> Another moon.

As the play unfolds there are apparent contradictions in the phases of moon and the time-span covering the action of the play. According to Theseus there will be four days of dark nights before the new moon and his wedding with Hippolyta, but during that length of time the lovers spend one night only in the moonlit wood. This is not an oversight on the part of the author but a deliberate ploy to differentiate our world of shadows, dependent upon the changing moon, and the world of the imagination existing far beyond such restrictions of time and place. The four days in the physical world pass during the darkness that lies between the waning of one moon and the rising of the next; this is the time of Hecate, the potential of the uncreated.

From darkness the scene changes to full moonlight, with the stage direction implied in Oberon's first words: 'Ill met by moonlight, proud Titania' (2.1.60). We have moved from the physical world to the world of mind outside time, where the moon gives light to the actions of the imagination and has a transformative effect on earthly beings: 'See the moon. . . instrument of nature, transforming matter below'.[1] It is within this world that the audience watches the path of love unfold, with all its pitfalls, according to the particular step the various protagonists have reached along their way.

Whilst it may be approached in many ways, at its highest level of understanding, *A Midsummer Night's Dream*, like all Shakespeare's plays, may be taken on the universal scale as a play created in the mind of God, in which all the worlds sport according to their diverse natures, alternating harmony with dissent. On the other hand, it may be seen as the growth of one particular man towards knowledge of himself. Theseus is a Duke, Shakespeare's indication that he has a noble mind and is therefore already of a high order. He is also a hero and a lover, with marriage approaching, and the play begins and ends at his court. And so in one respect, the lovers, the fairies and the mechanicals may be seen as the multifarious aspects of the personal worlds of Theseus himself, and the entanglements of the young lovers as the dreams of his own imagination through which his soul comes into harmony with his beloved.

For Theseus still has much to learn about love. He passes the harsh sentence on Hermia that, if she does not make the loveless marriage desired by her father, she must either die or become a nun. His query of concern to Hippolyta as they leave, 'What cheer, my love?' (1.1.122), clearly signifies that she has been looking unhappy about his verdict. The sadness of his higher soul, with whom he is about to be unified in marriage, underlines the fact that he has not yet understood the full meaning of love and compassion.

So Theseus is responsible for the lovers' entry into the wood which, in its twists and turns, becomes a maze, much like the mythical labyrinth through which he had to travel in order to find the Minotaur. A labyrinth represents the path of pitfalls that the creative imagination holds for a lover, and so these lovers, both as characters in their own right and as the journeying soul of Theseus, stumble their way towards the light of day and the enlightenment of the Promethean fire.

The first exchange between Lysander and Hermia, while they are still in the material world of the court, demonstrates the strength of their love and that they are, indeed, made for each other, despite her father's objection. Lysander's declaration that 'The course of true love never did run smooth' is followed by a list of possible obstacles raised against love: the difference in age or status, the pressure of family and friends, war, death or sickness. All are pitfalls on the path of love and, during Lysander's speech, Hermia's interjections—'O cross!. . . O spite!. . . O hell' (1.1.134–40)—serve to emphasise that here, in the unknown darkness of the moon where Hecate rules at the crossroads, they need to make a decision. While Lysander speaks of their love disappearing into the jaws of darkness, Hermia sees with more clarity that destiny has put an obstacle in their path in order to prove the truth of their love:

> If then true lovers have been ever cross'd,
> It stands an edict in destiny.
> Then let us teach our trial patience,
> Because it is a customary cross,
> As due to love as thoughts and dreams and sighs,
> Wishes and tears, poor fancy's followers.
>
> 1.1.150–5

Hermia knows the difference between true and false love. She understands that love bestowed on the wrong person is a result of fancy and can only lead to sighs and tears. True love, on the other hand, is a condition of the soul that has to be tested, and therefore the trials of love should be borne with patience.

In her role as the heavenly part of Lysander's soul, Hermia has pointed him in the right direction. Agreeing it is their destiny that they should be put to the test, he proposes that, after first meeting in the wood, they should elope to his aunt's house where they will be married. Hermia swears her love by its most powerful images, thereby setting out the path to be followed by the true lover:

> I swear to thee by Cupid's strongest bow,
> By his best arrow with the golden head,
> By the simplicity of Venus' doves,
> By that which knitteth souls and prospers loves,
> And by that fire which burn'd the Carthage queen
> When the false Trojan under sail was seen.
>
> 1.1.169–74

The lover first receives the arrow in the heart and falls physically in love. Learning virtue and the purity of Venus' doves, he proceeds to the world of the soul where he finds union with his beloved. Finally the Promethean fire of the angelic mind draws him to the divine light. In the image she gives here of the Carthage queen, the fire is that of the funeral pyre on which Dido throws herself when she is deserted by Aeneas. Ironically this foreshadows the faltering of Lysander's love, while Hermia, like Dido, remains as true as the Promethean fire.

It is in the wood, in the world of the imagination, that Lysander's love is to be tested, proving his constancy. The test is performed not through Cupid's dart itself, for he has already been pierced by that before the play starts, but by the result of its deflection. Oberon tells Puck how the arrow of love, the ray of divine light and beauty, was once aimed by Cupid at a chaste priestess and, missing its mark, buried itself in a white flower. Assuming the properties of the arrow, the flower changed colour from virgin white to the deep purple of passion. The ray of beauty had been deflected from its original virginal target to the purple of consummated love. In the terms of the gods, it had passed from Diana to Ceres, from the new moon to the full, another reason why the wood is flooded with moonlight. The juice of the flower, when placed in a lover's eye, enables him to look beyond physical appearance to the beauty of soul. But, because the flower was penetrated by a deflected arrow, it also arouses physical passion for an object of love that may not be true for that lover.

With the juice of the flower applied to his eyes, Lysander's love is deflected from Hermia to Helena and he appears to fail his test of constancy. However, he sees through Helena's outward appearance to the beauty of her heart:

> Transparent Helena! Nature shows art,
> That through thy bosom makes me see thy heart.
>
> 2.2.103–4

He then believes that his true soul has been revealed to him by reason:

> Reason becomes the marshal to my will,
> And leads me to your eyes, where I o'erlook
> Love's stories, written in love's richest book
>
> 2.2.119–21

Helena is not, of course, Lysander's true soul-mate, but his experience of seeing beyond her external appearance to the beauty of her soul enables him, with the second application of juice, to see Hermia in the light of her own true beauty. Although he was temporarily inconstant, his vision of the true beauty of heart enables him, when he leaves the wood, to be raised by the heavenly Venus into the fulfilment of marriage and union with his soul.

Helena reveals her understanding of love when we first meet her. She has lost the love of Demetrius, who is now fascinated by Hermia's beautiful appearance. She bewails his attraction to the false light that for him shines in Hermia's eyes and, in a beautiful speech on Platonic love, she speaks of the heavenly Venus who dwells in the world of the angelic mind. This love looks beyond the physical form and sees the true beauty hidden within. As Helena says, she admires not so much Demetrius' looks but his qualities, that is his virtues which are found in the world of the soul:

> How happy some o'er other some can be!
> Through Athens I am thought as fair as she.
> But what of that? Demetrius thinks not so;
> He will not know what all but he do know;
> And as he errs, doting on Hermia's eyes,
> So I, admiring of his qualities.
> Things base and vile, holding no quantity,
> Love can transpose to form and dignity:
> Love looks not with the eyes, but with the mind,
> And therefore is wing'd Cupid painted blind.
>
> 1.1.226–35

While Lysander is deflected from his love during the action of the play, Demetrius has already lost his way before the play begins. The physical attractions of Hermia are, for him, a step on the downward path. The effect of the juice on his eyes is, therefore, to direct them back to their true objective and, at the same time, to open them to heavenly love. As Oberon squeezes the love juice on his eyes, he asks that the soul of Helena will now 'shine as gloriously / As the Venus of the sky' (3.2.106–7), and indeed Demetrius' first words on seeing her are addressed to a goddess: 'O Helen, goddess, nymph, divine!' (3.2.137).

The Two Gentlemen of Verona, probably written a year or so before the *Dream*, contains a similar situation. Proteus, unable to appreciate more than Julia's outward beauty, rejects her for Sylvia, from whom he learns virtue and the meaning of heavenly beauty. Although, unlike Demetrius and Lysander, he needs no love potion to recognise the beauty of soul, Sylvia enables him to return to his true beloved, the constant Julia:

> But Sylvia is too fair, too true, too holy,
> To be corrupted by my worthless gifts.
>
> 4.2.5–6

In her long speech above, Helena speaks of the transformative effect that love on the initiatory path may have on the beloved:

> Things base and vile, holding no quantity,
> Love can transpose to form and dignity.

Bottom and his fellows, artisans working with their hands, are rooted in the physical world. Again it is because of Theseus that they enter the Athenian wood at night, this time in order to rehearse for a play that they hope to present at his wedding feast. As the physical world is adorned by nature, so the mechanicals may be seen as the traits of Theseus' nature that have to be tamed into harmonious forms before the soul may be unified; self-aggrandisement like Bottom's lowers his standing in the physical world and needs to be brought under control. Whilst bearing this in mind, Bottom should also be considered as a character in his own right, whose pomposity leads to his transformation into an ass. He is in fact greatly privileged for he is given an opportunity to learn from his experience and rise a little above the lower state of man, for which he has been named Bottom. As a result of the deflected juice that Oberon has placed in Titania's eyes, he becomes the misplaced object of her love. The juice also has the same effect on her as on the lovers, allowing her to see his inner beauty and look beyond his outer form. Her love effects a further transformation in him which, when he is returned to the human state, enables Bottom to take his place on the stage before the Duke in the part of a famous lover, Pyramus. As 'all the world's a stage' (*As You Like It*, 2.7.139), Bottom has begun to act the lover on the stage of life—although, since he plays Pyramus on an actual stage, which is even further removed from reality than the physical world, he is but a shadow of a lover.

Nevertheless, all the indications are that he has been given that part as a preparation for setting off on the true path of love.

Having been put into a charmed sleep, Bottom awakes from his night of love with the fairy queen overwhelmed by the memory of his dream, a most rare vision, which in the world of the imagination is a reality. He is unable to describe it but his muddled phraseology conveys that it is beyond all sensory experience:

> I have had a most rare vision. I have had a dream, past the wit of man to say what dream it was. Man is but an ass if he go about to expound this dream. Methought I was—there is no man can tell what. Methought I was—and methought I had—but man is but a patched fool if he will offer to say what methought I had. The eye of man hath not heard, the ear of man hath not seen, man's hand is not able to taste, his tongue to conceive, nor his heart to report, what my dream was.
>
> 4.1.203–12

His confusion and euphoria over his experience is not surprising for he has spent a night with a goddess, waited on by daemons.

The fairies are the daemons of nature, spirits who inhabit the world directly beyond men, to whom they are closely linked. Ficino writes in *De Amore*:

> Daemons involve themselves very closely and zealously in taking care of the affairs of the lower creatures, especially human beings. Because of this service, all daemons seem good.[2]

As the fairies gather to bless the house of Theseus at the end of the play, Puck speaks of the threefold goddess of nature whom they serve:

> And we fairies that do run
> By the triple Hecate's team
> From the presence of the sun,
> Following darkness like a dream . . .
>
> 5.1.369–72

As the queen of the fairies, Titania is a daemon of nature, but she also carries all aspects of the triple goddess. There is no doubt that she has the status of a divinity for, besides the fairies who serve her in the wood, she has her own priestesses in the mortal world. When she speaks of her little Indian boy, over whom she and Oberon are quarrelling, she refers to his mother as 'a votress of my order' (2.1.123). Her name, Titania, relates her to Hecate who, as the chaos from which creation arose, was one of the early race of gods known as the Titans. In her relationship with Hippolyta, the huntress, and the dominant symbol of the play, the moon, she is Diana. At the same time, with the sentence of everlasting winter that she has conferred on the earth, she is Ceres, the mother goddess who cast the same spell over nature when her daughter, Persephone, was held prisoner in the underworld by Hades. The image of Titania laughing with her pregnant priestess as she copies the movements of the big-bellied sailing ships, further identifies her with the goddess of the full moon, filled with the bounty of nature:

> When we have laughed to see the sails conceive
> And grow big-bellied with the wanton wind;
> Which she, with pretty and with swimming gait
> Following (her womb then rich with my young squire),
> Would imitate, . . .
>
> 2.1.128–32

A comparison has often been noted between Bottom and Lucius, the hero of *The Golden Ass,* written by the philosopher Apuleius during the second century AD. In a dream, when like Bottom he had been changed into an ass, Lucius was visited by the Egyptian goddess Isis, who calls herself Nature, the universal Mother.[3] As a moon goddess she is related to the triple goddess of nature, but the Romans who adopted her also equated Isis with Venus. Titania has something of all these forms: as a fairy she is a daemon, as the queen of the fairies she is the triple goddess of nature and, in her highest form as the goddess of love, she is Venus. So, during his night with Titania, Bottom's asinine nature is imbued with the love of the goddess of love herself. On a universal scale, the whole night of love between Titania and Bottom celebrates the marriage of heaven and earth. No wonder Bottom is so dumbfounded when he awakens from his 'dream'!

It is natural that the parts of Titania and Hippolyta, and of Theseus and Oberon, are often played by single actors, for there is a strong link between the characters. One of the causes of the fairies' quarrel is their mutual jealousy of each other's relationship with their mortal counterparts. As Ficino says above, daemons involve themselves very closely and zealously in taking care of the affairs of the lower creatures, especially human beings. While Oberon orchestrates the movements of all the mortals who visit the wood that midsummer night, he is the particular daemon of Theseus, just as Titania is that of Hippolyta. The friction between the fairies shows that their mortal counterparts are not yet ready for the concord of marriage. Disharmony in heaven reflects discordance in the world and, as we saw in Chapter 3, the anger of the gods reveals itself in the natural world as strange phenomena against its own laws. Titania, recounting these natural disasters, refers particularly to the anger of the moon, the physical form of the triple goddess that dominates this play. As Titania is also, in one of her aspects, that goddess, she is herself both the cause and the effect of the disharmony manifested in the events she describes:

> Therefore the moon, the governess of the floods,
> Pale in her anger, washes all the air,
> That rheumatic diseases do abound.
> And through this distemperature we see
> The seasons alter: hoary-headed frosts
> Fall in the fresh lap of the crimson rose;
> And on old Hiems' thin and icy crown,
> An odorous chaplet of sweet summer buds
> Is, as in mockery, set; the spring, the summer,
> The childing autumn, angry winter, change
> Their wonted liveries; and the mazed world,
> By their increase, now knows not which is which.
> And this same progeny of evil comes
> From our debate, from our dissension;
> We are their parents and original.
>
> 2.1.103–17

Theseus is responsible for both the lovers' and the mechanicals' presence in the wood, his verdict having been the cause of the elopement and his marriage celebrations the reason for the play that Bottom and his friends wish to rehearse. On the other hand Oberon, as the daemon of Theseus, determines the events that will take place in the world of the imagination. In 1611, when Ben Jonson and Inigo Jones' masque *Oberon* was performed at court, King James' elder son, Prince

*Costume design
for Prince Henry
as Oberon by
Inigo Jones,*
Oberon, *1611*

Henry, played the title role. He was considered to be noble in virtues and, as the heir to the throne, all the hopes for a new golden age were invested in him. Although the masque was performed fifteen years after the *Dream*, it seems that both authors perceived Oberon to be the fairy form of Theseus. Jones' design shows a character that might at first sight be taken for Theseus, a soldier in breastplate and plumed helmet. A closer look reveals that he is adorned with creatures of nature: the head of a bird over his brow, a satyr on his chest and the masks of lions on his boots and left shoulder.

In his highest form, Oberon is Pan, the god of nature, of whom Francis Bacon wrote: 'The ancients have, with great exactness,

delineated universal nature under the person of Pan.'[4] Oberon works
through the vagaries of nature, personified by his servant Puck, who
embodies all the mischief and mistakes made by man according to
earthly nature. Puck is imbued with the spirit of Mercury, full of
mischief and laughter, who, with Mercurial speed, can 'put a girdle
round the earth in forty minutes' (2.1.175–6). Puck, when he is Mercury
in his lower form, becomes a hobgoblin who takes delight in caus-
ing discomfort by toppling old ladies from their milking stools and
leading the lovers through brambles and briars. In his higher form,
Puck as Mercury is the messenger of the gods who brings the spirit of
love in the form of the purple flower to the lovers. His lower aspect
confuses the issue by placing the juice in the eyes of the wrong lover,
but the higher rights it in the end!

Inigo Jones' design for Oberon signifies not only his role as Pan but
also his warrior aspect as a Mars figure contrasting with the love of
Venus represented by Titania. The resolution of the uneasy relationship
between Theseus and Hippolyta is reflected in the quarrel between
Titania and Oberon, or Venus and Mars, over the little Indian boy. He
was the child of the priestess who Titania adopted after her death, till
he was stolen from her by Oberon. Mythologically, the offspring of
Venus and Mars, love and strife, is Harmonia. The little Indian boy
represents both the harmony that has been disrupted and the harmony
in which both couples are finally united. During the course of the play
both Oberon and Titania have become more kindly in their natures.
Oberon grows in compassion for the lovers and Titania gives gener-
ously to a creature who, to use Helena's words above, is 'base and
vile, holding no quantity', but whom, through her love, she is able
to 'transpose to form and dignity'. Her generosity continues when
she finally relinquishes the child to Oberon and the heavenly and the
natural world come together in harmony. As usual this is signified with
music as they dance together:

> Sound, music! Come my queen, take hands with me,
> And rock the ground whereon these sleepers be.
>
> 4.1.84–5

The sleepers, rocked into harmony by the dance of the fairies, are
awakened by Theseus and Hippolyta passing that way on a hunt. Now,

with the full understanding of love, Theseus quickly overcomes the protests of Egeus that his daughter should marry a husband of his choice and declares that both sets of lovers should be married that day, at the same time as he is to wed Hippolyta:

> For in the temple, by and by, with us,
> These couples shall eternally be knit.
>
> 4.1.179–80

The world of the imagination having accomplished its transformations, the action returns to Theseus and his court where all three pairs of lovers are married, having passed the test of the soul. The wedding takes place in the temple of Diana, goddess of the new moon that has now risen in the sky. Tonight their love will be consummated, but first they are to be entertained by a play that, through humour, depicts the world of shadows from which they have escaped. The performance of *Pyramus and Thisbe* by Bottom and his friends brings the action firmly down to earth. Lacking any in its actors, it requires strong imagination on the part of the audience:

HIPPOLYTA: This is the silliest stuff that ever I heard.
 THESEUS: The best in this kind are but shadows; and the worst are
             no worse, if imagination amend them.
HIPPOLYTA: It must be your imagination then, and not theirs.
 THESEUS: If we imagine no worse of them than they of themselves,
             they may pass for excellent men.

> 5.1.207–12

On a stage upon a stage, a shadow of the physical world that is itself but a world of shadows, a well-known tragedy is played as farce. The story of lovers forbidden to marry by their parents, meeting by arrangement at an appointed spot, is identical to the first part of Hermia and Lysander's story but, whereas their story has a happy ending, Pyramus and Thisbe undergo a fate similar to Shakespeare's tragic lovers, Romeo and Juliet. In this enactment, however, any potential for tragedy is turned to farce, anchoring itself firmly in the body of the world. Here life is tangled like their speech: 'a tangled chain,' says Theseus, 'nothing impaired but all disordered (5.1.124–5). The moon, too, is but a shadow of her reality. She appears neither in the form of the goddess in the sky nor as a personification of the goddess herself, but as a shadowy portrayal of the Man in the Moon. Cast in the part, Starveling the tailor carries the traditional stage properties of lantern, thorn-bush and dog.

The play ends in the harmony of a dance. When the lovers retire to bed, the fairies arrive to dance around the house, casting moonlight to bless their unions and their future offspring. The new moon of the virgin goddess, Diana, will shortly grow to the full moon of Ceres, and nature, it is to be hoped, will be bountiful.

For Shakespeare, a dream is a vision that takes place in the imagination. It is still a shadow of reality but brings a clearer perception of truth than the information gained through the senses when we are apparently awake in the mundane world. When the gods wish to prophesy or advise, they always appear in a vision or a dream. Pericles has first to fall asleep so that Diana may appear in a vision, directing him to her temple where Thaisa will be found and, towards the end of *Cymbeline*, Posthumus lies asleep in prison so that Jupiter may arrive on his eagle and deliver his prophesy that all will be well in the end. It was also, of course, the vision of a goddess who appears in Bottom's dream.

Earlier in Posthumus' dream his dead parents and brothers come to appeal for the god's help, for dreams often convey the wishes of dead mortals as well as the gods. In *The Winter's Tale*, when Antigonus lands on the shore of Bohemia with Hermione's baby daughter, he tells how she appeared to him in a dream and asked that her child be named Perdita:

> Come, poor babe:
> I have heard, but not believ'd, the spirits o' th' dead
> May walk again: if such thing be, thy mother
> Appear'd to me last night; for ne'er was dream
> So like a waking.

3.3.15–19

The nocturnal visitors are not all benign, for dreams often entertain the ghosts of those who have been murdered. The guilt of Caesar's murder lies so heavily on Brutus that he is unable to sleep; nevertheless, the ghost of Caesar appears to his heightened imagination. On the eve of his final battle, Richard III has numerous visitors who taunt him in his sleep, but the same ghosts give promises of support in the battle to the peacefully sleeping Richmond:

GHOST OF PRINCE EDWARD
TO KING RICHARD: Let me sit heavy on thy soul tomorrow.
How thou stab'st me in my prime of youth
At Tewkesbury; despair therefore, and die.
TO RICHMOND: Be cheerful, Richmond, for the wrong'd souls,
Of butcher'd princes fight in thy behalf;
King Henry's issue, Richmond, comforts thee.

5.3.119–24

Richard dies before his dreams can act upon his imagination but, in one of the most famous dreams in Shakespeare, when Lady Macbeth is sleepwalking, her dream enhances the physical reality. The vision of the whole murder of Duncan is re-enacted in her fevered imagination until the obsession with the blood on her hands plunges her into the dark chaos of Hecate and madness ensues.

On the path of love, it is possible to find the spark of divine light even in the darkest situation, the highest being reflected in the lowest. Shakespeare shows it on stage as the lighted taper that Lady Macbeth holds in her hand. It is interesting that, in such a dark play as *Macbeth*, this light should still be found, even in this tiny physical form. When the shadows are dispersed, such a spark might be seen in its full beauty as the Promethean fire, the light of divine beauty. It is this quality of the Creator that first draws the love of each unmanifest world towards the higher world so that, through their union, it may itself become manifest. On the return journey, the lover is drawn to the beauty of each world of his beloved, beginning with the shadowy world of her outward beauty, which increases in radiance as he begins to recognise beauty of soul and mind. In the following sonnet Shakespeare is addressing heavenly beauty, which he sees with more clarity when the senses are dulled in sleep. The greatest vision would be to see the form of beauty herself, lit by her own radiance, but until then dreams by night give him a clearer vision of beauty than her shadowy appearances in the daylight of the physical world:

When most I wink, then do mine eyes best see,
For all the day they view things unrespected;
But when I sleep, in dreams they look on thee,
And, darkly bright, are bright in dark directed.
Then thou, whose shadow shadows doth make bright,
How would thy shadow's form form happy show
To the clear day with thy much clearer light,
When to unseeing eyes thy shade shines so!
How would, I say, mine eyes be blessed made
By looking on thee in the living day,
When in dead night thy fair imperfect shade
Through heavy sleep on sightless eyes doth stay!
All days are nights to see till I see thee
And nights bright days when dreams do show thee me.

                                        Sonnet 43

CHAPTER ELEVEN

Twin Souls

So we grew together,
Like to a double cherry, seeming parted,
But yet an union in partition,
Two lovely berries moulded on one stem;
So, with two seeming bodies, but one heart.

Dream 3.2.208–12

———•◦•———

ELENA, FINDING herself, instead of Hermia, the object of both young men's love, believes her friend has conspired with them in order to spite her. In the speech above, she reproaches Hermia, reminding her of their former closeness, that they were twin souls having two bodies but one heart. Like Helena, Celia in *As You Like It* chooses to remain close to her twin soul, Rosalind, and goes with her into banishment:

We still have slept together,
Rose at an instant, learn'd, play'd, eat together,
And whereso'er we went, like Juno's swans,
Still we went coupled and inseparable.

1.3.69–72

In those plays where two young women such as these are close to one another, they represent not only their own lover's soul but also the soul in a wider context, so on the symbolic level Hermia and Helena are united as the soul of Theseus. While Hermia represents the beauty of form that first attracts the lover, the beauty of soul is personified by Helena, both aspects of the heavenly and earthly Venus. After the many pulls of nature, the desires and confusions represented by the experiences of Lysander and Demetrius during their night in the Athenian

113

wood, both forms of beauty are loved and the soul comes finally into harmony with itself.

The beautiful appearance of Rosalind has likewise attracted Orlando and it then becomes her function to tutor her lover in how to love her soul by disguising her physical form. Celia, on the other hand, has no teaching to perform, for she becomes the recipient of a true love instantaneously realised as each step along the path is accomplished in no time at all. On the universal scale, they are the daughters of dissenting fathers who are brothers. Rosalind's father is the true duke, a spiritual role which cannot be filled unlawfully, whilst Celia's father is the usurper. Only by the usurping soul following and joining in love with the true soul, as Celia follows Rosalind to join her father in the forest, may the banished duke be restored and heaven reign again on earth.

In some plays, the twin souls are actually twins by birth. In *Twelfth Night* they are of different sexes. Viola, like Rosalind, has to disguise her appearance until Orsino understands her to be his true love and recognises her beauty of soul. He relinquishes the mistaken object of his love, Olivia, to Sebastian. As Viola's twin, Sebastian is also a twin aspect of Orsino's soul and therefore symbolically transforms the false to true love when he accepts Olivia's offer of marriage. As Orsino himself is the duke, it is not only the individual worlds of the man which become unified, but also the universal worlds of heaven and earth.

The Comedy of Errors is a play with two pairs of twins, or twin souls, that is worth exploring in more detail. One of its chief sources is a Roman play, *Menaechmi* by Plautus. Using its idea of twins and the confusions arising from their mistaken identity, Shakespeare furthers the complications by introducing their twin servants, the Dromios. With these two pairs of twins separated at birth, Shakespeare creates a scenario that shows the divided worlds of man being reunited. Ficino writes how these worlds may come together only through love:

> But love attracts like to like. Individual pieces of earth adhere to other pieces of earth like themselves because of reciprocal, joining love. . . Similarly, drops of water move toward each other, and, with the whole body of water, toward a place appropriate to them.[1]

Thus, when Antipholus of Syracuse, the twin who makes the first move by setting out to find his brother, lands in Ephesus, he explains his desire for reunion in the same terms:

> I to the world am like a drop of water
> That in the ocean seeks another drop,
> Who, falling there to find his fellow forth,
> (Unseen, inquisitive) confounds himself.

1.2.35–8

When the Antipholus twins are bound to the ships' masts in the great sea storm that also separates their parents, they are tied not together but each with his servant, Dromio—the name derived from the Greek word meaning fleet of foot. The two Dromios are aptly named for they spend much of the play running errands. Since the physical world is the most moveable of all the worlds, being the world where action takes place, and the Dromios are earthy by nature, they represent the bodily parts of their masters and their reunion at the end of the play symbolises union within the corporeal world. It is just as well that each master and servant was bound together to the same mast for it would be difficult for either Antipholus to locate his twin without a physical body!

The Antipholus twins represent a divided soul. When Antipholus of Syracuse first enters, having arrived from Ephesus in search of his brother, the First Folio edition describes him as Antipholus Erotes, thus identifying him with erotic love, the lower Cupid ruled by the earthly Venus. The two Venuses are combined within Cleopatra and harmonise at her death as the heavenly Venus alone, while in *The Comedy of Errors* the soul is represented by twin lovers drawn in opposite directions by the two powers of Cupid. Antipholus Erotes of Syracuse sets out on his quest at the earthly level, for the inn where he lodges is named the Centaur. A mythical creature, half man and half horse, the centaur is a symbol of the baser instincts, the lustful part of earthly love.

In contrast, Antipholus of Ephesus lives at a house named the Phoenix, the mythical bird whose continual rebirth in the fire of love represents the heavenly Venus. However, neither brother remains in his appointed sphere; rather, as the play progresses, each gains something of the other until they become so well balanced in love that the Cupids of the twin souls are united as one.

Antipholus of Ephesus, although his marriage and the name of his house indicate that he has made some progress on the path towards divine love, shows through his behaviour that he has still much to learn of constancy and virtuous living. His relationship with his wife, Adriana, is uneasy and, having been barred from entering his own house by the presence of his twin, whom his household, including his wife, has mistaken for himself, he flies into a fury. His friend, Balthazar, urges him to protect his reputation and the unviolated honour of his wife but, determined to teach Adriana a lesson, he runs to the arms of a courtesan at the Porpentine—the name of the inn means porcupine or spiny pig, like the centaur a symbol of licentiousness. Meanwhile, as one twin is failing his test in virtue and constancy, the other is being entertained in heavenly love at his brother's house, the Phoenix.

So the positions of the two brothers have been reversed: one has moved from the Centaur to the heavenly love of the Phoenix while the other has been precipitated from the Phoenix to the earthly delights of the Porpentine. And while his brother dallies with the courtesan, Antipholus of Syracuse meets and recognises heavenly love. His twin's sister-in-law is a character not present in the Roman original; Shakespeare has introduced her deliberately to be the heavenly Venus whose beauty awakens love for the divine. For Luciana means 'light', that same light of divine love, or Promethean fire, that lovers see sparkling in the eyes of their beloved. It is God's ray that Ficino saw lighting the beauty of all the worlds:

> But just as a single ray of the sun lights up four bodies, fire, air, water, and earth, so a single ray of God illuminates the Mind, the Soul, Nature and Matter. And just as anyone who sees the light in those four elements is looking at a ray of the sun itself and, through that ray is turned to looking at the supreme light of the sun, so anyone who looks at and loves the beauty in those four, Mind, Soul, Nature and Body, is looking at and loving the splendour of God in them and, through this splendour, God Himself.[2]

Seeing Luciana, Antipholus of Syracuse recognises her as 'more than earth divine' (3.2.32) and, by addressing her as 'mine own self's better part' (3.2.61), he acknowledges her as the higher part of his soul. Already the sight of her is having a transforming effect and he rightly asks, 'Are you a god? Would you create me new?' (3.2.39). As she is of the divine world, her eye and her heart are clearer and dearer and he sees her as his heavenly counterpart:

> It is thyself, mine own self's better part,
> Mine eye's clear eye, my dear heart's dearer heart,
> My food, my fortune, and my sweet hope's aim,
> My sole earth's heaven, and my heaven's claim.
>
> 3.2.61–4

His description of her as a mermaid, spreading her golden hair over the silver waves, recalls the beauty of the heavenly Venus in Botticelli's *Birth of Venus*, a painting inspired by Ficino's *Commentary on Love*. His longing for union with her is the same as desire for union with his soul:

> Sing, siren, for thyself, and I will dote;
> Spread o'er the silver waves thy golden hairs,
> And as a bed I'll take thee, and there lie,
> And in that glorious supposition think
> He gains by death that hath such means to die;
> Let love, being light, be drowned if she sink.
>
> 3.2.47–52

Having made a pun on the lightness of love, he follows it with Ficino's analogy of the sun for the Promethean fire: 'gazing on your beams, fair sun' (3.2.56).

Another important addition to the source play is the golden chain. The divine ray of light that penetrates and connects all the worlds is often spoken of by Platonists as the golden chain. In his *Hymenaei*, Shakespeare's contemporary and friend, Ben Jonson, refers to this link between the worlds as a golden chain let down from Heaven.[3] In a marginal note he cites Homer as his source, also Macrobius, the fourth-century Neo-Platonist who quotes Homer on the connecting chain between God and the universal worlds:

> . . . since mind emanates from the Supreme God and Soul from Mind, and Mind, indeed, forms and suffices all below with life. . . the close observer will find that from the Supreme God to the bottommost dregs of the universe there is one tie, binding at every link and never broken. This is the golden chain of Homer which, he tells us, God ordered to hang down from the sky to the earth.[4]

Antipholus of Ephesus has promised his wife, Adriana, a gold chain, although she is doubtful whether she will ever receive it. In the following speech, as she confides in her sister, she describes it in such a way as to show that she recognises its significance as an emblem of divine love. In the second line, some editors have emended the Folio's 'alone a love' to 'alone a toy'. The former is clearly Shakespeare's intention, for Adriana is hoping that her husband will remain true to her and the union of their souls' marriage will be consolidated and drawn by the golden chain towards divine love. But sadly she fears that he is unable to recognise and love the true gold of her virtuous soul, even though her physical beauty may be fading:

> Sister, you know that he promised me a chain;
> Would that alone a love he would detain,
> So he would keep fair quarter with his bed:
> I see the jewel best enamelled
> Will lose his beauty; yet the gold bides still
> That others touch, and often touching will
> Wear gold, and no man that hath a name
> By falsehood and corruption does it shame.
> Since that my beauty cannot please his eye,
> I'll weep what's left away, and weeping die.
>
> 2.1.106–15

If only he would remain true to his wife, in the closeness of their marriage bed he would discover the true gold of her virtue. In one of his letters Ficino uses the same analogy of gold for the beauty of soul:

> . . . when our Plato discoursed on beauty. . . it was beauty of soul he sought from God, which he called wisdom and most precious gold. When this gold was given to Plato by God, it shone in him most brilliantly, because he was so pure in heart.[5]

Immediately following the above speech from Adriana, Antipholus of Syracuse enters with the news that Dromio has left his gold safely at the Centaur. On one level it is the gold he brought with him to pay for his expenses while searching for his brother, on a spiritual level it is the gold or true beauty of his soul that will help to restore him to himself. The divine ray of love has been rooted at the start of his journey from the Centaur: in other words, the end of the golden chain is fastened, in the words of Macrobius, 'to the bottommost dregs of the universe'.

Having promised the gold chain to his wife, Antipholus divorces himself from Adriana, and any hope of heavenly love, by offering it to the courtesan. Adriana, again conversing with her sister, recognises that, through their separation, her husband is creating a division, between them and within himself, from the undivided love of God:

> O, how comes it,
> That thou art then estranged from thyself?
> Thyself I call it, being strange to me,
> That undividable, incorporate,
> Am better than thy dear self's better part.
>
> 2.2.119–23

In the end, neither Adriana nor the courtesan receive the chain, for their Antipholus has lost all contact with the ray of love. Instead, it is his brother who, as soon as he leaves Luciana, is given the chain by the goldsmith, Angelo—surely, with such a name, a messenger from the angelic world! Everyone Antipholus of Syracuse meets wishes to shower him with gifts and he rejoices in his good fortune. Through finding his heavenly Venus, he has earned these benefits, but they also prove what his twin has lost. He is a man of good reputation in the city but, owing to his recent behaviour, he is in danger of losing it. The last straw is to be arrested for the theft of a chain which he never received. While his brother is offered gold at every turn, he loses both the chain and the gold sent by his wife to bail him out.

Although tempted to stay and woo Luciana, Antipholus of Syracuse believes that she must be a siren in a land of witchcraft, for this is the only explanation he can find for the extraordinary behaviour of the citizens of Ephesus. He therefore decides to escape. However, he is confronted by the angel, Angelo, over his rightful possession of the gold chain and is forced to fight for his honour, a quality of the angelic mind. With both honour and chain intact, he escapes with his Dromio into the Priory, the house of God. Having rooted the chain in the depths of the physical world, he ascended through love to the world of the soul at the Phoenix and now, still wearing the chain, is taken to the divine world of the Priory.

Characters from the heavenly world frame the action of the whole play. In the opening scene, Egeon, the twins' father, explains the earlier events of the shipwreck to the Duke of Ephesus. The dukedom shows him to be a representative of God on earth, but the duke's name, Solinus, is significant too, for 'sol' or the sun is also the physical light of God:

> What then is the light of the sun? It is the shadow of God. So what is God? God is the sun of the sun; the light of the sun is God in the physical world, and God is the light of the sun above the intelligences of the angels.[6]

Egeon, whose name is taken from the Aegean Sea, is also from the realm of the gods. Both he and the duke, the light of God, frame the action of the play: they appear at the beginning and do not return to the action until the last scene, when Egeon is reunited with his wife, the mother of the Antipholus twins. As the Abbess of the Priory into which her son escapes, she, too, is a regent of God, belonging to the angelic world. She calms the excited throng and reprimands the agitated Adriana before reuniting with her children, their servants and her husband. Parents, sons and servants, representing the three worlds of mind, soul and body, are joined as one.

The twin souls have also found their twin loves. The difficulties encountered by Antipholus of Ephesus in his marriage have been resolved through his misfortunes and, having learned his lesson, we can assume that he will now appreciate the love, loyalty and virtues of his wife. His brother, having briefly usurped his place in the Phoenix household, has found heavenly love. Between them they have experienced both the heavenly and the earthly Venus and now, while on one level both will find true marriage with their soul-mate, on another all four represent the unified soul.

The union of the soul through the sons also releases the parents. Throughout the play, Egeon has been held in chains and his wife has been incarcerated in a priory, both symbolic of being bound to the physical world. Now they can break free and in joyful reunion return to their marriage in the heavenly world. Reunited with their sons and their Dromios, all are linked in a golden chain and the universe is in harmony with itself.

In the final scene Shakespeare brings us, the audience, back to earth by giving the last lines of the play to the Dromios. We may have had only intimations of the higher worlds but we can at least be free to leave the theatre with laughter in our hearts and, like the Dromios, go hand in hand. Twins with two bodies and one soul in harmony,

> We came into the world like brother and brother,
> And now let's go hand in hand, not one before the other.

CHAPTER TWELVE

The Dark House

Love is merely a madness, and I tell you, deserves
as well a dark house and a whip as madmen do.
                    As You Like It, 3.2.388–9

S HAKESPEARE'S LOVERS aspire to return to the source of their
being, drawn by the beauty of its blazing light, the Promethean
fire. But if, like Macbeth, they act against their nature to such an
extent that they are drawn through the material world to the grossest
level of existence, the light dwindles to barely a glimmer in the darkness
of original chaos. Herein lies Hell or Hades and here Shakespeare's
tragic heroes are confronted with their actions. It is not the intention
of this book to look closely at Shakespeare's tragedies but, in covering
all areas of the Platonic worlds, it is necessary to consider how he deals
with this underworld of darkness.

Plato wrote famously of a cave in *The Republic* where the shadows
of people and objects, reflected by a fire onto its walls, are believed by
those in the cave to be the things themselves. This is an analogy of the
images of imagination, the outward appearance of the true forms that
lie in the world of the angelic mind. Throughout the preceding chapters
it has been made clear that Shakespeare laid much stress on the importance of mistrusting outward appearances. Ficino gives an analogy of the
creation as a design for a building existing in the mind of the architect.
The true form lies as an idea in the divine intelligence, that is, the
angelic mind or heavenly world, and manifests in the mundane world
through the imagination, where it is but a shadow of its real self:

As the design of a whole building and of its parts exists in the
mind of an architect, so the design of this whole world and of its

parts exists in the divine intelligence beyond the world. That world beyond he calls the world of intelligence, and eternal; this world he calls the world of senses, and temporal. The models of things in this world he calls ideas in the divine intelligence, and the resemblances of the divine intelligence in this world he calls images and shadows.[1]

In this context it is worth repeating the sonnet that was quoted in the chapter on constancy. There it was said that the constant heart to which this sonnet is addressed is the stability of the soul when it becomes one with the angelic mind. Shakespeare is describing, not the physical beauty of a young male lover, nor a dark lady, but divine beauty, the beauty that Ficino said human beings knew face to face before they became imprisoned in the body and to which they long to return. It is the beauty of the One whose imagination creates ideas, emotions and finally the shadowy bodies of the physical world. There are millions of beautiful forms that are only shadows of the divine beauty who *lends* them to the world; the beauty of Helen or Adonis is but a shadow of the beauty of their creator:

> What is your substance, whereof are you made,
> That millions of strange shadows on you tend?
> Since every one hath, every one, one shade,
> And you, but one, can every shadow lend:
> Describe Adonis, and the counterfeit
> Is poorly imitated after you;
> On Helen's cheek all art of beauty set,
> And you in Grecian tires are painted new.
> Speak of the spring and foison of the year,
> The one doth shadow of your beauty show,
> The other as your bounty doth appear;
> And you in every blessèd shape we know.
> In all external grace you have some part,
> But you like none, none you, for constant heart.
>
> *Sonnet* 53

The dark cave, in which the shadows get darker and the matter denser the further one advances inside, is an analogy of the physical world that has cropped up time and time again and has become part of universal consciousness. Zoroaster is said to have consecrated a cave to Mithras, the father of all things, to represent the world he created. Porphyry, the third-century AD Platonic philosopher, wrote a treatise on a cave, first mentioned by Homer, called the Cave of the Nymphs, which he compares with the world:

> The world therefore with great propriety may be called a cave; agreeable indeed, at its first entrance, on account of its participation of form, but involved in the deepest obscurity to the intellectual eye which endeavours to discern its dark foundation. So that its exterior and superficial parts are pleasant, but its interior and profound parts obscure: and its very bottom is darkness itself.[2]

Containing the darkness of the unknown, caves have always exerted a fearful attraction. Leonardo da Vinci, a follower of Ficino's Christian-Platonism, wrote in his *Notebooks*:

> . . . two contrary emotions arose in me, fear and desire. . . fear of the threatening dark cavern, desire to see whether there were any marvellous things within it.[3]

As the place where the soul enters its physical body, there are indeed many marvellous things to be seen in the world and, in his painting of *The Virgin of the Rocks*, Leonardo depicts Christ's descent into the material world by placing the Virgin and Child within a cave.

Those who penetrate deep into the darkness of matter and manage to keep their reason (for in these areas one may easily loose one's wits and suffer the lunatic fantasies that conjure up 'more devils than vast hell can hold') may still come face to face with chaos, the formless darkness from which we are created. But they are never completely lost, for the spark of love that drew the unformed mind to the love of God, although buried in the darkness, still faintly flickers. The highest light is reflected in the deepest dark for, in the well-known utterance of Hermes Tristmegistus:

> What is below is like what is above, that the miracle of the one thing may be accomplished.[4]

So it is not surprising to find that Shakespeare too uses the symbol of the cave for the physical world, although his caves are not always

Leonardo da Vinci, Virgin of the Rocks, *National Gallery, London*

designated caves and are therefore easy to overlook. They may be any dark, enclosed spaces that are cave-like, such as Malvolio's dark house, Gertrude's closet or Lear's hovel.

King Lear loses sight of his light of love when he rejects Cordelia and she leaves for France. His mind dissolves into madness as he descends through the material world into the chaos of unformed matter. His descent may be compared with the journey of Orpheus into the underworld to recover his lost love, Eurydice. Lear's approach is through a storm in which all nature appears to be disintegrating and the very body of the world is flattened into primary chaos. This external tempest is also taking place within himself as his arrogant nature is thrown into turmoil and finally disintegrates.

Although battered by the storm and full of self-pity, he begins to find pity within himself for others, first of all for the Fool:

> Poor fool and knave, I have one part in my heart
> That's sorry yet for thee.
>
> 3.2.72–3

Kent, in disguise as Lear's servant, leads him to shelter from the storm in a hovel. As he enters this symbolic cave of the shadowy world, Lear's compassion is stirred again for his fellow human beings, the 'poor naked wretches' (3.4.28) who are in the same plight as himself. He has begun to find within himself the spark of love that was lost and it is from this point that his soul starts on its regenerative path. In the hovel they meet another madman, Gloucester's son, Edgar, now disguised as Poor Tom. He is a man of good and pure nature, true to his father, by whom he has been unjustly banished. Gloucester's blindness to the wicked lies of his bastard son, Edmund, about Edgar's loyalty, results eventually in his own physical blindness. At the same time, Edgar assumes the role of rejected love and, renamed Poor Tom, descends into the darkness of the cave. Love returns to Gloucester when Edgar eventually returns to guide his blind father back to life by staging a mock death and rebirth on the cliffs at Dover.

Earlier, both Lear and Edgar are maddened by the evil wrought against them by their respective families and their view of creation is one of darkness and despair. Lear can see nothing of the world now except its gross matter, stripped of any ornament of nature. Mankind becomes no more than the physical body and he strips off his clothes in an effort to return to what at this moment he believes all men to be, 'a poor, bare, forked animal'. Deep in the darkness of the underworld, the Fool hastens to wrap him in his cloak, and speaks of the spark of light:

> Now a little fire in a wild field were like an old lecher's heart; a small spark, all the rest on's body cold. Look! here comes a walking fire.
>
> 3.4.109–11

The walking fire is, in fact, Gloucester with a torch, arriving to lead them to better lodgings, one step at least out of the underworld. It is like the candle that Lady Macbeth keeps by her constantly after the murder of Duncan, even as she is sleepwalking; for, although she has fallen into the furthermost limits of hell, she is seeking still a glimmer of the Promethean fire by which she may be guided.

Poor Tom, having lost his wits in the underworld, is beset by luna- tic fantasies of the 'foul fiend'. To him the appearance of Gloucester is not as the divine spark but 'the foul Flibbertigibbet' who 'squinies the eye'. On the other hand, to Lear's chaotic mind, Edgar appears to be a philosopher whose wisdom helps him through his sojourn in the innermost cave. When Gloucester rescues them from the hovel, Lear insists, 'I will keep still with my philosopher' (3.4.173). Not only Gloucester but also the distorted wisdom of this mad philosopher has helped the return of his soul from the underworld for, in Poor Tom, Lear has found the counterpart of Cordelia, his rejected love. It should also be remembered that Kent, his constant heart, although hidden by a disguise, has been in faithful attendance.

Hamlet also rejected love for if, as his father's ghost had asked, he was to avenge him, there could be no room for love in his heart. With the rejection of Ophelia, Hamlet is drawn further and further into the darkness until he is faced with his mother, in Latin 'mater', from which we get 'matter'. The material world gave him his physi- cal birth and it is only by penetrating the dark recesses of this world that he will be able to find salvation. This gives greater significance to the question, 'Now, mother, what's the matter?' (3.4.7) that he asks on entering the womb-like cavern of her closet to look into the face of his own substance. In truth he is looking deep into the closet of his own heart. So when Gertrude cries, 'Oh Hamlet... thou turns't mine eyes into my very soul' (3.4.88–9), it is his own voice speaking.

Now, having reached to the depths of his soul, he may discover the heights. Face to face with the mother or matter of his being, he can begin to rediscover the spirit of love, lost when he rejected Ophelia. But first a confrontation must take place. His rage at her marriage so soon after the death of his father breaks loose at last and he reviles her union with such a devil as Claudius, the antithesis of his noble father:

> A murderer and a villain,
> A slave that is not one twentieth part the tithe
> Of your precedent lord, a vice of kings . . .
>
> 3.4.96–8

At the height of his passion, the ghost of his father reappears. Although he has tried to obey the spirit's plea for revenge and, in preparation, has forsaken love, he now recognises the ghost of his father as a spirit of darkness. Realising that he needs heavenly protection, he appeals to his guardian angels:

> Save me and hover o'er me with your wings
> You heavenly guards.
>
> 3.4.104–5

Only Hamlet can see the ghost for he is now deep in the underworld himself, dangerously near madness. Frightened by his unnatural behaviour, Gertrude cries:

> Alas, how is't with you,
> That you do bend your eyes on vacancy,
> And with th'incorporal air do hold discourse?
> Forth at your eyes your spirits wildly peep,
> And, as the sleeping soldiers in th'alarm,
> Your bedded hair, like life in excrements,
> Start up and stand on end.
>
> 3.4.116–22

The ghost is altogether milder than when he first appeared to Hamlet on the battlements. It is now Hamlet who first mentions revenge,

'Do you not come your tardy son to chide?' The ghost affirms that he should not forget 'his almost blunted purpose', but his concern is more for the mother and her need of care and compassion, so he asks Hamlet to 'step between her and her fighting soul' (107–13).

The conflict is also within Hamlet's soul, into which now enters a renewed glimmer of love and compassion. The ghost's countenance evokes a feeling of pity from Hamlet, and his soul, having resolved to take the path of revenge and blood, realises the alternative of tears and compassion: 'tears perchance for blood' (3.4.130). At this point, the ghost, representing that part of Hamlet's soul which had decided to follow the path of revenge rather than love, disappears never to return. Hamlet's words to his mother are now far more compassionate as he pleads for her to repent and to promise never to go to bed with Claudius again. In this speech to his mother he addresses the darkness within himself:

> Confess yourself to heaven,
> Repent what's past, avoid what is to come;
> And do not spread the compost on the weeds
> To make them ranker.
>
> 3.4.151–4

She replies, 'Oh Hamlet, thou hast cleft my heart in twain', to which he answers,

> Oh throw away the worser part of it
> And live the purer with the other half.
>
> 3.4.158–60

For Hamlet too, the purer part of his soul begins once more its ascent and the idea of revenge, that has no place in the spiritual world, dissolves. Although his soliloquy, 'How all occasions do inform against me' (4.4.32), after his encounter with Fortinbras and his army on their way to England, ends with renewed thoughts of revenge, there is good evidence that the scene was added during early performances and then cut as not representing Shakespeare's original intention.[5] Hamlet has progressed beyond such thoughts by this time for, in the closet/cave of his mother, a spark of the Promethean fire has penetrated the darkness.

Prometheus was among the Titans, forerunners of the Olympian gods who are associated with the mundane world where the forms of the angelic mind have multiplied into a great variety of particular images: the name Titan is derived from a Greek word meaning 'particular'. Feeling sorry for mankind, 'the poor, bare, forked animals' who lived without fire, Prometheus stole the fire of the gods. As a punishment he was bound to a rock, where every day an eagle pecked at his liver and every night it was regenerated.

Prometheus serves the lower orders of mankind, those attached to material things who have not yet seen the blaze of the heavenly world or the light of inner beauty. But this light may not be given to human beings unless they desire it, and they cannot desire it if they do not know it is there!

A mortal has to be in a fit state to love and receive the divine fire; Cupids carrying flaming torches as well as bows and arrows are part of Renaissance iconography. But if the fire is taken unlawfully it rises quickly heavenwards, home to its divine source, and anyone who tries to snatch love without earning it becomes, like Prometheus, chained fast to the cave-like rocks of the material world.

One who tries to seize love while in no fit state to receive it is the arrogant steward, Malvolio, in *Twelfth Night*. Malvolio has presumed to love beyond his station by aspiring to marry Olivia. None but those whose intentions are pure are ready to embark on winning the Promethean fire of such beauty as Olivia's. Hers is the beauty of the heavenly Venus but Malvolio seeks only the earthly Venus; he is greedy for her sexual favours but even more for his own advancement in the material world. Ficino quotes Plato as saying that this form of love is due to ignorance of its true meaning:

> Plato says that this form of love is born of human sickness and is full
> of trouble and anxiety, and that it arises in those men whose mind
> is so covered over with darkness that it dwells on nothing exalted,
> nothing outstanding, nothing beyond the weak and transient image
> of this little body. It does not look up to the heavens, for in its black
> prison it is shuttered by night.[6]

In the earthly world of shadows, nothing is as it seems and Malvolio has to learn not to trust appearances, as he trusted the letter by which he was duped into believing Olivia loved him. And so, having tried to steal the heavenly fire of love, he is punished by being bound and imprisoned in a dark house. This is Plato's black prison shuttered by night, the dark recesses of the earthly cave. The scene has often been criticised for being cruel and beyond a joke, but, when it is understood why Shakespeare wrote it as he did, its significance becomes clear.

Feste visits Malvolio in the dark house, deceiving him with the illusion of being the priest, Sir Topas. Deep in the darkness of matter, it requires the imagination of the angelic mind to see the divine spark. Feste, with the wisdom of the fool, tells him that the house does have apertures to the light but they are blocked, for the bay windows are as transparent as barricades and the clerestories have as much lustre as ebony. The soul has windows for truth to enter if we do but choose to see them and this darkness, says Feste, is but ignorance of the truth.

FESTE: Sayst thou that house is dark?

MALVOLIO: As hell, Sir Topas.

FESTE: Why, it hath bay windows transparent as barricadoes, and the clerestories toward the south-north are as lustrous as ebony: and yet complainest thou of obstruction!

MALVOLIO: I am not mad, Sir Topas. I say to you, this house is dark.

FESTE: Madman, thou errest. I say there is no darkness but ignorance, in which thou art more puzzled than the Egyptians in their fog.

MALVOLIO: I say this house is as dark as ignorance, though ignorance were as dark as hell; and I say there was never man thus abused.

                                                              4.2.35–48

Malvolio has suffered the dark house but he has not seen the Promethean fire. The spirit of darkness stays with him and turns him over, like Hamlet, to the spirit of revenge. He leaves the stage at the end of the play with the cry, 'I'll be revenged on the whole pack of you!' Olivia, on the other hand, in the spirit of love, counters this with compassion, 'He has been most notoriously abused' (5.1.377–8).

The four great tragic heroes all owe their downfall to a hardening of the heart and the rejection of love. This leads to the dark house where, unless like Hamlet and Lear they find a spark of the Promethean fire of

love to guide them back to the light, they are doomed to eternal darkness like Macbeth. Othello is faced with the extinction of this light as
he wrestles over his decision to murder Desdemona. She is the higher
part of his soul, the divine beauty that lights all his worlds. If he puts
out the earthly flame of the candle, it can be re-lit, but if her body dies
even the true Promethean fire cannot bring it back to life:

> It is the cause, it is the cause, my soul,
> Let me not name it to you, you chaste stars:
> It is the cause, yet I'll not shed her blood,
> Nor scar that whiter skin of hers than snow,
> And smooth, as monumental alabaster;
> Yet she must die, else she'll betray more men,
> Put out the light, and then put out the light:
> If I quench thee, thou flaming minister,
> I can again thy former light restore,
> Should I repent me; but once put out thine,
> Thou cunning pattern of excelling nature,
> I know not where is that Promethean heat
> That can thy light relume.
>
> 5.2.1–13

Othello will not return from the underworld in this life but Shakespeare always ends on a positive note. Full of remorse, Othello kills
himself and dies with a kiss on Desdemona's lips, a symbol that there
is reunion after all, even in death.

CHAPTER THIRTEEN

Rebirth and Reunion

———•◦•———

T HE CAVE that appears in *Cymbeline* has a more pleasant aspect, although even this has its dark depths which have to be penetrated so that the soul may be reborn. It lies in the Welsh mountains near Milford Haven where Belarius has hidden the twin sons of King Cymbeline whom he stole as infants. Here, in the womb of the created world, Guiderius and Arviragus have been reared as hunters and sportsmen, strong in limb with the innate grace of the princes they truly are. Unconfined to the cave, they roam the wild, mountainous countryside of the natural world. The doorway to the cave is both an entrance to the darkness within and the exit to the light beyond. While Imogen, on finding the cave for the first time, enters it timidly, with drawn sword, Belarius emerges with these words to the princes:

> A goodly day not to keep house with such
> Whose roof's as low as ours! Stoop, boys: this gate
> Instructs you how t'adore the heavens; and bows you
> To a morning's holy office.

> 3.3.1–4

Belarius refers to the princes as 'sparks of nature' (3.3.79), for the divine light is not only apparent in their own nature but they themselves represent the goodly nature of their father, Cymbeline. He lost sight of true love when he married his second wife and, under her influence, banished his daughter's husband from his court.

As with other fathers such as Lear and Leontes, Cymbeline's daughter, Imogen, represents the world of the soul and the love he has lost. Imogen is referred to, in the prophecy that Jupiter makes to Posthumus, as 'a piece of tender air' (5.4.140) and it will be remembered that, in the model of Inigo Jones' worlds described in the first chapter, the higher soul is associated with the element of air. While each of Shakespeare's characters have their own level of being, they may also represent the being of the protagonist, which lifts the action onto a universal level. Here it is Cymbeline, as the title of the play and his own position as king suggests, even though he appears to play a comparatively small part in the action.

Having despatched the husband, Cymbeline and his queen try to marry Imogen to the Queen's son, Cloten, a lumpish, foolish creature who personifies ignorance. Imogen receives a letter from her banished husband, Posthumus, and flies to meet him at Milford Haven. However, because of the evil schemes of Iachimo, Posthumus believes her to have been unfaithful and instructs his faithful servant, Pisanio, in whose protection he has left her, to kill her. Imogen now carries the double burden of rejected love; she is the lost soul of both father and husband. Travelling dressed as a boy, the common disguise for the hidden soul, she stumbles upon the cave where Belarius and her unknown brothers live. On first seeing her, they recognise her divine beauty shining through her travel-stained disguise:

> By Jupiter, an angel! Or, if not,
> An earthly paragon! Behold divineness
> No elder than a boy!

> 3.7.15–17

So divine light enters the cave, like Prometheus bringing the heavenly fire to earth. But her light is almost quenched and lost love nearly dies. She feels unwell and, believing it to be a remedy, takes a poison which the Queen had given to Pisanio and he had passed on to her. Devastated at finding her dead in their cave, Belarius and the brothers perform a sacred rite over her body. Placing her body with her head to the east, the direction of the rising sun and thus symbolic of rebirth, they sing and strew her with flowers. However, as soon as they leave, she stirs into life. Although her restoration was due to the faithful doctor who, mistrusting the Queen, had mixed a potion that gives only the appearance of death, its underlying meaning is that of the rebirth of the soul. It also coincides with Posthumus' repentance for his treatment of Imogen. Shakespeare emphasises the significance of this moment with the sacred rite performed by the two brothers. Faith also plays a part in ensuring that love is reborn, the faith of Pisanio and Imogen's own fidelity to her husband, in recognition of which she has named herself, as a boy, Fidele.

A macabre twist is that when she awakens she finds the headless body of Cloten, who has been killed by Guiderius, placed by her side. Love has not yet the strength to recognise the falseness of outward appearances: she believes the headless body, dressed in her husband's clothes, to be Posthumus himself. Becoming distraught, she is rescued by the leader of the Roman forces in Britain and taken into his service. The name of the Roman is Lucius, or light! The divine spark has been rekindled in the soul and, after a battle against the Romans that ends in a peaceful settlement, Imogen and Posthumus are reunited, together with Cymbeline and his sons.

Posthumus, whom Cymbeline banished, represents the qualities and virtues of the angelic mind. Born after his father's death as his name indicates, his full name is Posthumus Leonatus, the lion-hearted. This noble name, inherited from his father, places him firmly in the heavenly world. He was born under the planet Jupiter, as the god himself tells Posthumus in a dream:

> Our jovial star reigned at his birth, and in
> Our temple was he married.
>
> 5.4.105–6

Ficino, writing on the influence of the gods on men, says that the angelic mind is called Saturn and Jupiter[1] and that they are the gods who represent existence and life. Inigo Jones' model of the universe depicts the angelic mind crowned by a fiery Jupiter.

His mother having died when he was born, Posthumus was taken into the protection of the king. There he earned the respect of all, as one of the gentlemen at Cymbeline's court describes in the opening scene:

> The king he takes the babe
> To his protection, calls him Posthumus Leonatus,
> Breeds him, and makes him of his bedchamber,
> Puts to him all the learnings that his time
> Could make him the receiver of, which he took,

As we do air, fast as was minister'd,
And in's spring became a harvest: liv'd in court
(Which rare it is to do) most prais'd, most lov'd;
A sample to the youngest, to th' more mature
A glass that feated them, and to the graver
A child that guided dotards.

1.1.40–50

So, close to the king, he is part of his family and therefore symbolically an aspect of his being. Ficino says that Jupiter strengthens the power of governing and ruling so it is not surprising that the new queen saw him as such a threat to her son's chances of gaining the throne, especially after he had married the king's daughter. Having been taken over by wickedness and ignorance in his new marriage, the first of Cymbeline's worlds to be rejected is the angelic mind and Posthumus is banished.

On a universal scale, Imogen is the world soul of the divine kingdom, represented by Cymbeline. But as the soul of Posthumus, his rejection of her and his desire for her death is even more terrible as they are man and wife and their union has been consummated. His soul does indeed appear to die but, with his repentance and the rebirth of his soul in the cave, they are reunited in the angelic mind through this beautiful image:

Hang there like fruit, my soul,
Till the tree die.

5.5.263–4

Following their own reunion, they are embraced by Cymbeline and his two sons, the good sparks of his true nature, denoting that all his parts have been reassembled and made whole. He is once again the King, the divine One. The dramatic image, five figures united on the stage, is significant, for five is the number of union. Jonson mentions this in *Hymenaei* as five candles are carried in a wedding procession:

For five the special number is,
Whence hallow'd Union claims her bliss.[2]

Jonson notes Macrobius again as his source:

The possession of unusual powers came to the number five because it alone embraces all things that are and seem to be. . . This number designates at once all things in the higher and lower realms. There is the Supreme God; the Mind sprung from his, in which the pattern of things are contained; there is the World-Soul, which is the fount of all souls; there are the celestial realms extending down to us; and last the terrestrial realm; thus the number five marks the total of the universe.[3]

It is not only a reunion of man as a whole, but also a reunion on the cosmic scale, when the Romans and Britons, the heart and mind of the universal worlds, enter into the harmony of universal peace. In the words of the soothsayer:

> The fingers of the powers above do tune
> The harmony of this peace.

> 5.5.467–8

It is no coincidence that the last word in this play, and the last word in the First Folio, is 'peace'.

The theme of death and rebirth is present in all Shakespeare's last plays. *The Winter's Tale* is particularly marked by its seasonal division of winter as the time of death and early summer as the time of rebirth, which Shakespeare denotes by the introduction of Time itself as a character. It should be noted that the title is not *A* but ***The** Winter's Tale*, signifying that it is not just one of the many tales told during the winter but is the tale of winter itself. It is the time of darkness when nature appears to have died although many seeds are germinating beneath the earth. 'A sad tale's best for winter' (2.1.25), says the young Prince Mamillius, but winter does not last forever and, in the second half of the play, spring produces the flowering of those seeds.

So on one level, *The Winter's Tale* is a play about nature, and not only the natural world but also the nature of mankind. But it is also, of course, a play about the journey of the soul, how the soul may fall into a dark misery of hell through the negative force of its own nature, and how it may regenerate through love and its own natural virtues. Richard III speaks of 'the winter of our discontent' (1.1.1.) and, in winter, jealousy takes over Leontes' soul and pulls him deep into the cave of the mundane world to the darkness of hell itself. In the spring his soul is restored to its rightful home of heavenly light.

Again the protagonist is a king, Leontes—like Posthumus a lion having the heavenly virtues of nobility and courage. Leontes and Hermione have been happily married for several years and their love is shown to have lasted: they already have one child and Hermione is again pregnant. So when Leontes believes she has been unfaithful to him, his terrible rejection of her is more damaging than the rejection of a lover before marriage. Since the mythological Hermione is the daughter of Mars and Venus whose other name is Harmonia, Shakespeare is emphasising the disruption of harmony in Leontes' soul when he reacts so strongly against her. Hermione's name also connects her with Hermes, who in one form is the messenger of the gods and, in his higher form, the one who carries the word of God.

Emotions, as everyone knows, can run amok if not controlled by reason and, in Leontes' irrational and sudden jealousy, Shakespeare illustrates only too well the power of an emotion uncontrolled by the reasonable mind. In our post-Freudian era we naturally tend to regard characters in a play from a psychological point of view and much Shakespearean criticism is built on that. But Shakespeare knew nothing of psychology; he was more concerned with the play of emotions within the cosmos of man and for him, when emotion turns from being a virtue to a vice, it is because love has been rejected. So, while a modern actor trained to reveal the psychological motivation of his character may find this sudden emotional switch of Leontes a problem, we should remember that Shakespeare was not interested in writing realistically: his characters *are* real people but they move within universal worlds.

Mad with jealousy, Leontes, the noble lion, falls into hellish darkness. Held fast in the grip of his insane passion, he makes three denials. In the Christian context, these may be compared with the three denials of Christ by St Peter. Against his true nature, he rejects first his wife who is the harmony of his soul, and then his new-born daughter. She is in the likeness of his nature and physical form, as Paulina is quick to point out when trying to persuade him the baby is his:

> Behold, my lords,
> Although this print be little, the whole matter
> And copy of the father;

> 2.3.97–9

and she continues with an invocation:

> Thou good goddess Nature, which hast made
> So like to him that got it.
>
> 2.3.103–4

Antigonus and his wife, Paulina, the true and faithful servants and friends of Leontes and Hermione, are ordered against their nature to carry out the lunatic demands of their master. First Leontes orders Paulina to commit his wife and daughter, the better parts of his own soul and nature, to the fire, a savage sentence reminiscent of the fires of Hell where now he finds himself. Then a degree of compassion returns and, ordering Hermione to be placed on trial, he tells Antigonus to take the baby to a remote and desert place and there abandon her.

His final rejection is of the oracle from Apollo. Although the messengers he sent to Delphi return with the pronouncement that Hermione is chaste, Leontes cries, 'There is no truth at all i'th' oracle' (3.2.140). This denial of the god invites immediate punishment. The words are no sooner out of his mouth than a servant enters with the news that his son is dead. In the enormity of his grief, Leontes at last realises the full measure of what he has done:

> Apollo's angry; and the heavens themselves
> Do strike at my injustice.
>
> 3.2.146–7

After making his three denials, Leontes' punishment is three-fold. The death of his son is quickly followed by Paulina's news that Hermione too has died. He has also lost his baby girl for, too late to be recalled, Antigonus has left for Bohemia to lay her on its shores.

Deep in the darkness into which his soul has plunged, he finds the spark of light. It is divinely given by Apollo, the god whose physical form is the sun and who in essence represents the divine light itself. Although the light arrives in the form of punishment, the deaths of his loved ones also illuminate Leontes' soul with the realisation of its true state. Hermione cannot be false. Brought to his senses, reason returns and, making a vow of repentance, Leontes dedicates his future life to shedding tears at the double grave of his queen and son. With repentance begins the regeneration of his soul. In the remembrance of what

'Hidden Truth brought forth by Time', title-page for *Francis Bacon,* New Atlantis, *1626*

once was and the love he has lost, Leontes is reborn and begins the long journey back from the dark night of his soul towards its reunification in harmony and love.

This is going to take time and, to help the audience fly over the next sixteen years, a winged personification of Time enters the stage to bridge the gap. Time spans the seasons from winter to early summer and the passage of time allows the travelling from Sicily to Bohemia; but it also takes time for the soul, hidden away like Hermione, to be reborn into the light, and the love that was lost—like Perdita, to be found. A contemporary emblem showing 'Hidden Truth brought forth by Time' is to be found on the title-page of Bacon's *New Atlantis.* The reborn soul, or truth, represented by a naked woman, is being drawn from a cave by Cronos or Time.

The whole of the fourth act passes in Bohemia, where Leontes' baby daughter has been found and brought up by kindly shepherds. Before Antigonus left her on the shore, Hermione appeared to him in a dream, instructing him to name her Perdita, she who is 'counted lost forever' (3.3.33). That which is lost is of course love, the love that Leontes now believes lies dead in Hermione's grave. But Leontes has spent the last sixteen years in repentance, so Perdita, although lost, is not lost forever. She has flowered into a beautiful girl whose role is to regenerate her father's reborn soul in the world of nature. From her descent into the darkness of winter, Perdita, like Persephone, is reborn to the world in the spring. She is even renamed Flora, the goddess of spring, by her lover, Florizel. She has been reared and nourished in the Arcadian world of Bohemia, a heavenly prototype of the natural world. Here the gods disport themselves, here Perdita is queen of the sheep-shearing festivities and now, in the early summer of her life, she falls in love. Her adopted family are good shepherds living close to nature and it is as a child of nature that she has been nourished and reared.

The sixteen years also bridge the worlds of tragedy and comedy and now, in the vein of all Shakespeare's comedies, the soul ascends the path of love. Florizel, the son of the king of Bohemia whom Leontes believed had betrayed him, is attracted by the beauty and virtue of Perdita and they fall in love. This stage of the lover's journey has not been reached only by Florizel but also by the regenerating soul of Leontes that now must re-enact each stage of the path if it is to ascend once more to union with its beloved. Thus the younger lovers re-enact the courtship of Leontes and Hermione that once preceded their union in marriage.

This ascent takes place in the angelic mind in the Arcadian world of the gods. Not only does Florizel address Perdita as Flora, but also, through his name, he is linked to the springtime goddess. He also compares himself to Apollo, the guiding god of the play, and Florizel acts as the light which draws Perdita, the love that was lost, back to Sicilia and her repentant father. After sixteen years of atonement, Leontes is ready to receive his regenerated soul; he is overjoyed when Perdita's true identity is revealed.

Paulina takes Leontes to see a statue of his dead wife and, as he says, his soul is pierced by her beauty. In the chapter on harmony it was pointed out that, whenever the heavenly and earthly worlds come together in the harmony of the soul, Shakespeare signifies the moment with music. So now, as Paulina calls, 'Music, awake her, strike' (5.3.98), the statue stirs into life. Leontes' reunion with Perdita ensured the restoration of his good and virtuous nature and now, as he takes the living Hermione in his arms, he is reunited with the higher aspect of his soul. The words of Polixenes and Camillo recall the image of Posthumus' reunion with Imogen:

> POLIXENES: She embraces him!
> CAMILLO: She hangs about his neck.
>
> 5.3.111–12

Whether Hermione has been alive and cared for by Paulina or whether she really died and has been magically resurrected is a question at the material level; the important point is that the soul was hidden until the moment came for its rebirth. As Hermione tells Perdita, she has preserved herself for this moment.

Hermes Tristmegistus wrote in his *Asclepius* of how Egyptian priests were able to bring statues to life by magically drawing down planetary influences. Ficino refers to him in *De vita coelitus comparanda* (*The Book of Life*) and compares the firing of an inert body with spirit to Prometheus, bringing the heavenly fire down to earth:

> Tristmegistus tells us of such things, too, which the Egyptians made out of certain things of the world in order to get strength. He says they used to bring the souls of daemons into these to good effect, including the soul of his ancestor, Mercury. In the same way, they used to make the souls of Phoebus, Isis, and Osiris descend into statues, to be made for men's use or even to be harmful to men. Likewise, Prometheus snatched life and heavenly light into a certain figment of clay.[4]

That this was well known in Renaissance England is supported by Shakespeare's contemporary, Francis Bacon:

> We are certain, from numerous figures and expressions of the ancients, that they judged the conservation, and in some degrees the renovation, of natural bodies to be no desperate or impossible thing.[5]

Whether the body is a statue, like Hermione, or an apparently dead body such as Imogen's, the ritual involved in bringing it back to life as part of the initiation of the soul is what is important. This theme in Shakespeare's late plays continues with the resurrection of another body in *Pericles*. The reunion of Pericles and his wife, Thaisa, in the temple of Diana[6] at the end of the play echoes that of Leontes and Hermione: there is an awakening of the higher aspect of the soul as it comes into harmony with itself in the angelic mind. Both wives are mothers removed from the world while their daughters re-establish the virtuous natures of their fathers; in both plays this takes sixteen years—until the daughters are of marriageable age. But, whereas Hermione is not actually resurrected until just before her reunion with Leontes, Thaisa is restored to life much earlier in the play and becomes a priestess in the temple during the intervening period.

The lifeless body of Thaisa, Pericles' wife who has been drowned at sea, is brought to the wise Cerimon, who practises a form of sympathetic magic. When the virtues and influences of the stars and planets, themselves forms of the gods, are drawn into particular plants, metals and stones and used correctly, they have healing properties. Believing there is a chance she may be revived, Cerimon calls for cloths to bring warmth to her body and fire to kindle her spirit. His knowledge of how to perform the magic of reviving a dead body came, as was quoted earlier, from the Egyptians:

> Death may usurp on nature many hours,
> And yet the fire of life kindle again
> The o'erpress'd spirits. I heard of an Egyptian
> That had nine hours lien dead,
> Who was by good appliance recovered.
>
> 3.2.84–8

Cerimon knows that a powerful way of bringing the influence of the gods to earth is by imitating the heavenly sounds of their physical forms, the music of the planets, in earthly music. In the same way that music is used to revive both Hermione and Imogen, so it is also summoned by Cerimon:

> Well said, well said; the fire and cloths.
> The still and woeful music that we have,
> Cause it to sound, beseech you.
> The viol once more! How thou stirr'st, thou block!
> The music there! I pray you, give her air.
> Gentlemen, this queen will live.
> Nature awaken a warm breath out of her.
> She hath not been entranc'd above five hours;
> See, how she 'gins to blow into life's flower again.
>
> 3.2.89–97

Through the physical warmth of cloth blankets, fire to kindle the spirit and music to bring harmony to the soul, life is reborn.

The last plays have the sense of another dimension: this is because they relate to the soul's final journey through the angelic mind. Before the soul is able to move freely in this world, it must be tested by descending deep into the darkness of its own beginnings to find the light therein—the true Promethean fire. This sparks the rebirth of the soul so that it may rise from its initiatory 'death'.

CHAPTER FOURTEEN

Set Me Free

PROBABLY THE LAST play that Shakespeare wrote without collaboration, *The Tempest* shows more clearly than any other of his plays how the work of the imagination in the angelic mind not only creates diversity but also draws the Platonic worlds together once more into one being. In his wholeness, Prospero has only to take the last step into the freedom of the One itself.

Leontes, Cymbeline and Pericles undergo a spiritual death and rebirth before reuniting with the higher parts of their souls in the angelic world. On the other hand, Prospero has been tested along the spiritual path before *The Tempest* begins, and audiences for the play witness a man in command of all the worlds, including the angelic mind, the world of the imagination. He has embarked on the final stages of initiation of the magus, the wise man, which are also the last steps on the path of love. By bringing all worlds into harmony within himself, he may at last become one with God.

Cerimon, the wise doctor in *Pericles,* was able to bring the influences of the planets to earth, through 'the blest infusions that dwell in vegetives, in metals, stones' (3.2.35–6), for the purpose of healing and even for raising the dead. He also believed that the study of the secret art of physic develops virtue and knowledge and leads to immortality. For, he says, it is virtue and knowledge rather than nobility and riches that make 'a man a god' (3.2.31). This is the art that Prospero has developed in order to achieve the same goal, to become a god. It would have been a heresy for Shakespeare to write this at the time but, in the Christian-Platonic tradition, the goal was not to become a lesser deity but God Himself. Prospero now has the power of all the lesser gods behind him to help him in his purpose. He is served by the power of the imagination, the creative force of both man and God. Through the imagination he can conjure all the characters and all the worlds of his own created island, as well as tempests and sweet music, nymphs and reapers, banquets and baying hounds.

Whilst it is important to stress that all the characters act according to their own natures as the action unfolds, and each reaches his own stage of development as an individual, nevertheless this play, perhaps more than any other, reflects the different aspects and worlds of one man. The tempest itself draws two important elements of Prospero's being onto the island. One represents his worldly part and the other plays the role of the lover. In his former life as the Duke of Milan, Prospero had spent too long over his books and the delights of study, 'thus neglecting worldly ends' (1.2.89), and had forgotten his mundane duties and responsibilities as Duke. This, as was found earlier, is a spiritual role to which Shakespeare gives as much weight as divine kingship; it is one that may not be discarded lightly. Antonio, Prospero's younger brother to whom he had relinquished the government of Milan, soon grew greedy and wished to seize absolute power. Prospero is caught in the maelstrom between the desire for knowledge and a desire for worldly power. Antonio opens the gates of Milan to the invading army of the King of Naples, with whom he has conspired against Prospero, and at the same time Prospero and his daughter are expelled from the city. His description to Miranda of their being hurried through the gates of Milan in the darkness sounds very like entering the portals of the underworld:

> . . . one midnight
> Fated to the purpose, did Antonio open
> The gates of Milan; and, i' th' dead of darkness,
> The ministers for this purpose hurried thence
> Me and thy crying self.

1.2.128–32

Cast adrift on a leaking ship, constancy comes to his aid: Prospero is helped by his faithful friend, Gonzalo, who provides plentiful supplies of food and clothes and ensures that his precious books are also on board. Prospero is accompanied by his three-year-old daughter, Miranda. She is well named the wonderful one (Latin, *mirandus*) for, Prospero's wife being no longer alive, Miranda is now the soul of her father. Unlike daughters in other plays who have taken on this role, she is neither lost nor banished, but remains with him, a light in the darkness and her father's salvation:

> O a cherubin
> Thou wast that did preserve me.
>
> 1.2.152–3

Sailing the seas is often used as a metaphor by Shakespeare for being cast forth on the sea of fortune. Although Fortune is a goddess, she pales into insignificance when compared with Divine Providence. This is the will of God Himself who, as Prospero tells Miranda, brought them ashore on the island: 'How came we ashore?' asks Miranda and her father replies, 'By Providence divine' (1.2.158–9). Ficino also calls divine providence 'angelic inspiration',[1] meaning the muse of fire that lights the creative imagination. For twelve years he has made a life here for himself and his daughter and now, after twelve years of study and good management of his island, he has prepared the ground of his intellect through sound use of his imagination.

Because Prospero has come under divine providence, fortune works in his favour, and so it is she who brings a ship close to the shores of the island, on which are travelling the King of Naples, his son and Prospero's brother, Antonio, the false Duke of Milan. Prospero, taking advantage of this opportunity offered by fortune, raises the tempest and casts all the passengers and crew unharmed onto the island. He is now at the height of his powers, he tells Miranda, and the time is ripe for him to move:

> I find my zenith doth depend upon
> A most auspicious star, whose influence
> If now I court not, but omit, my fortunes
> Will ever after droop.
>
> 1.2.181–4

He says nothing more at the time but, as the play unfolds, it is apparent that he means to bring the various strands of his life together, to make amends where he may and to draw together in love all aspects of himself, all his worlds.

The creative power of his imagination is Ariel. Prospero repeatedly

calls him his Spirit and, as his name implies, the First Folio lists him
among the names of the actors as 'an airy spirit'. He is one of the
daemons, spirits which, according to Ficino, are closely linked to
mankind;[2] Ficino also said that Hermes Tristmegistus 'composed'
through aerial demons.[3] As a spirit he has no form, or rather he may
assume any shape he chooses, moving invisibly through the air. However, as Prospero has power over all the elements, so may his servant
Ariel command them at his will. Since fire rules the angelic mind, it
is the chief element and, in its highest form, the true Promethean
fire, it is the creative ray of God. Ariel describes himself as this form
of creative fire when telling Prospero of his exploits in raising the
tempest:

> I flam'd in amazement: sometimes I'd divide,
> And burn in many places; on the topmast,
> The yards and boresprit, would I flame distinctly,
> Then meet and join.

1.2.198–201

Amazement has come to mean incredulity or bewilderment, but it is
used here in the biblical sense of overwhelming wonder at a manifestation of the divine. So Ariel's description of himself as flaming 'in
amazement', suggests that he is divine fire at work.

When Prospero arrives on the island he hears the groans of Ariel,
imprisoned for twelve years in a pine tree by the evil witch, Sycorax,
who has since died. Here is another image of the interior depths of
the cave of the physical world. The power of his imagination has been
imprisoned and the free use of his higher mind impeded for so long
because of a lack of balance. By turning inwards to his books, he has
neglected his responsibilities to the world and his dukedom, the kingdom of God. There should be a proper balance of all the worlds and
this starts to be righted when, having faced death in his leaky boat, he
is safely cast up, reborn through divine providence, on the shores of the
island. Now his imagination may be freed and Ariel put to his proper
use. The pine tree is also a symbol of immortality so, by setting Ariel
free, Prospero leaves the restriction of the mortal body to enter the
freedom of the immortal world of mind. But he needs his imagination,
his 'Art', as he calls it, to fulfil his purpose, and Ariel may not be entirely

free until the final stages of Prospero's spiritual journey are complete.

Antonio and Sebastian, the King of Naples' brother, still acting according to their natures, scheme to kill the king while he is asleep, but Prospero, working through Ariel, stays their hand and wakes Gonzalo, his faithful and loving friend, who was also aboard the ship. Here the power of the angelic world awakes faithful love, which intercepts the evil deed.

Later, as Antonio and Sebastian are again planning to kill the king, Prospero conjures up strange shapes that magically produce a banquet to which they invite the hungry and thirsty shipwrecked courtiers. Prospero is described as being 'above and invisible' during this performance, an apt stage direction for someone who is working from a heavenly point of view. The courtiers are tempted to eat but, before they can make a start, Ariel appears as a harpy. According to Greek legend, the harpies were creatures with the faces of beautiful women and the wings and talons of eagles, sent by the gods to torment the blind Phineus by whipping away any meal set before him. Ariel follows suit: clapping his wings, he makes the banquet disappear. They are in a world where outward appearance is as insubstantial as a dream and their credulity is tested to its limits. Ariel then berates them for supplanting Prospero and exposing him and his child on the sea, finally telling Alonso that his son is dead. This leaves them in a distracted state but still within Prospero's power, so that which was undesirable in his own nature may be controlled:

> My high charms work,
> And these my enemies are all knit up
> In their distractions: they now are in my power.
>
> 3.3.88–90

The other two intend to fight the fiends, but Alonso, appalled and incensed, says he will seek his son in the underworld:

> Therefor my son i' th' ooze is bedded; and
> I'll seek him deeper than e'er plummet sounded,
> And with him there lie mudded.
>
> 3.3.100–2

They also have their own paths to follow and, as madmen in the realm of fantasy seeing 'more devils than vast hell can hold', descend into the underworld. Here they may hope to find the spark of light in the darkness that will lead them to redemption. Like Malvolio in the dark house, Ariel confines them, unable to move, in a 'lime-grove'. 'Lime' suggests 'limbo'—being held in a state of suspended animation; it also alludes to bird-lime, used as a trap for snaring small fowl and a metaphor favoured by Shakespeare for the bait of love. In Chapter 9 the illustration was given of Beatrice being baited like a fish by her friends, so that she will fall in love with Benedick, and later in the scene the sporting metaphor continues with Ursula's line, 'She's lim'd, I warrant you! We have caught her, madam' (*Much Ado* 3.1.104).

When he is ready to be merciful and they are penitent, Prospero sends for the king and the two conspirators. His 'nobler reason', or reason of the higher mind, tells him that he must forgive and this action, more rare than vengeance, he is prepared to take:

> Though with their high wrongs I am struck to th' quick,
> Yet with my nobler reason 'gainst my fury
> Do I take part: the rarer action is
> In virtue than in vengeance: they being penitent,
> The sole drift of my purpose doth extend
> Not a frown further. Go release them, Ariel:
> My charms I'll break, their senses I'll restore,
> And they shall be themselves.
>
> 5.1.25–32

The divine spark arrives in the form of Ariel to rescue the wrong-doers and they are led before Prospero to receive forgiveness for their sins. The 'ignorant fumes that mantle their clearer reason' are chased away by their 'rising senses' (5.1.66–8) and they become 'themselves'. So now, in the state of being themselves and purged of sin, they are fit, if they so desire, to embark on their own path of love. On the other hand, viewing them as aspects of Prospero, he is freed from the worldly part of his nature by forgiving its darker side. It is at this point that Prospero puts on the garments of the Duke of Milan: he also becomes 'himself' but, while the others are only at the beginning, he is at the end of his spiritual journey. The difference is that he knows he is himself, that he is the Duke, the universal man.

After his faithful friend, Gonzalo, had ensured that Prospero's books and material comforts were aboard the leaking boat, he had remained at the side of the false duke. Now, shipwrecked on the island with him, the King of Naples and his brother, he has been their constant companion. However, because of his earlier compassion, he is not magically imprisoned in the lime-grove with the rest, but weeps to see his comrades so frozen in time. Once again, faith has helped to bring the darker aspects to the light.

The other important passenger on the shipwrecked boat is Ferdinand, son of the King of Naples. He has not been drowned, as Ariel led his father to believe, but was miraculously saved like all the others. His is the role of the lover, that part of Prospero that embarked on the journey of the soul so many years before. Prospero was unified with his soul at the time of his marriage but, when his wife died, Miranda inherited the role of her father's soul. It is up to her and her lover Ferdinand to take Prospero's soul into the heavenly world, where it will finally be united in the One.

Since the first task of the soul is to unify its earthly and heavenly aspects, and as water is an element of the earthly part, Ariel dresses as a water nymph in order to lead Ferdinand to Miranda, the heavenly air. Thus Inigo Jones depicts Juno, the air, ruling the world of the soul; Iris, the rainbow among the rain-clouds, represents the mixture of water and air where earth and heaven meet. Ferdinand is drawn by Ariel's music, the harmonising factor used by Prospero throughout this play. For his own part, as a lover setting foot on the path, he is caught by this 'bait' and drawn by the beauty of the music:

> Where should this music be? I' th' air or th' earth?
> It sounds no more: and sure it waits upon
> Some god o' th' island.

> 1.2.390–2

He recognises it as heavenly music, 'No mortal business, nor the sound / That the earth owes' (1.2.409–10), and it leads him straight to the 'goddess on whom these airs attend' (1.2.424–5). Face to face with Miranda, his goddess and the beauty of his soul, he straightway falls in love. On both his own and Prospero's behalf, he is tested harshly at first. Prospero starts him off on his path with physical labour, carrying logs. Willingly undertaking the task in the cause of love, he meets Miranda again. Their declaration of love for each other is observed by an invisible Prospero, Ferdinand's alter ego. Having first fallen in love with her outward beauty, he is now in love with her virtues and the beauty of her soul:

> Admir'd Miranda!
> Indeed the top of admiration! Worth
> What's dearest to the world! Full many a lady
> I have ey'd with best regard, and many a time
> Th' harmony of their tongues hath into bondage
> Brought my too diligent ear: for several virtues
> Have I lik'd several women; never any
> With so full soul, but some defect in her
> Did quarrel with the noblest grace she ow'd,
> And put it to the foil: but you, O you,
> So perfect and so peerless, are created
> Of every creature's best!

3.1.37–48

All his words now ring with the true sound of the lover, but it is Miranda who proposes marriage to him, the heavenly part of his soul offering herself in union. They join hands as a symbol of their forthcoming marriage and Prospero, silently rejoicing at their love, allows Ferdinand to leave his earthly manual work to prepare himself for the heavenly work ahead.

Later, Prospero enters with the two lovers and, telling Ferdinand that all his labours were but trials of his love, he gives Miranda to him as his future wife, 'a third of mine own life' (4.1.3). This is an affirmation that she is his soul, one of his three worlds of body, soul and mind. Having warned Ferdinand that she must remain chaste until she is married, Prospero summons up the gods from the heavenly world of his imagination to perform a masque for the lovers.

When *The Tempest* was performed at court in 1611, it was as part of the festivities to celebrate the marriage between the King's daughter, Princess Elizabeth, and Frederick, the Elector Palatine, and it has often been proposed that Shakespeare added the masque for this occasion. But the entertainment that Prospero conjures up for Miranda and Ferdinand is so integral to the action that I don't believe Shakespeare would have written the play without it. It is not a wedding ceremony, as in *As You Like It*, but it clearly signifies that Ferdinand and Miranda are about to be unified in the world of the soul.

Prospero has just elicited from Ferdinand a promise that he will not sleep with Miranda until they are married, that nothing will ever melt

> Mine honour into lust, to take away
> The edge of that day's celebration
>
> 4.1.28–9

and the importance of this is heavily stressed by Prospero and as strongly avowed by Ferdinand. It is important that no step on the path of love is omitted: symbolically the consummation of love, the actual union of body and soul, may take place only after the ritual of marriage has been performed. It will be remembered from preceding chapters that there are two Venuses: the heavenly beauty, whose power draws the lover to God, and the earthly Venus, who leans towards the delights of the flesh. If, after falling in love with outward beauty, the lover succumbs to the earthly Venus before he can take the next step of pursuing a virtuous life, he will not reach the world of the soul. Ferdinand, having fallen in love with Miranda's beauty, has been put to a test of love through heavy manual work. He has made no complaint but, before he is allowed to become unified with his bride, the heavenly part of his soul, he has still to prove his other virtues, one of them being patience. The masque is a ritual that will help Ferdinand recognise the true qualities of the soul.

It begins with music and the appearance of two goddesses, Iris, the rainbow, who bridges heaven and earth, and Ceres, the goddess of earth's abundance. Iris calls on Ceres to attend Juno, a third goddess and queen of the heavenly world of the soul whose name, as Ben Jonson pointed out in *Hymenaei*, is an anagram of 'unio' or union. She is about to arrive with her peacocks, a symbol of unity since the many colours of their plumage appear to merge into one. In his setting for *Hymenaei*, Inigo Jones showed her seated on a golden throne between two peacocks.

Ceres asks Iris the whereabouts of Venus, whom she has not seen since the goddess of love plotted her daughter Persephone's abduction by Hades. Iris assures her that Venus has flown away with her doves,

more symbols of love. Apparently she and Cupid have been thwarted in
an attempt to draw a couple into making love before marriage. Clearly
Iris is referring to the earthly Venus whom Ferdinand and Miranda
have rejected under the orders of Prospero. Now Juno descends and
blesses the couple's union, while Ceres promises 'earth's increase' for
their offspring and future abundance. Ferdinand appreciates the harmony of the masque and asks Prospero if the actors are spirits:

> This is a most majestic vision, and
> Harmonious charmingly. May I be bold
> To think these spirits?

To which Prospero replies that they are spirits summoned by the art
of his imagination:

> Spirits, which by mine Art
> I have from their confines call'd to enact
> My present fancies.
>
> 4.1.118–22

The masque ends in a dance, with naiads, the nymphs of water, and
reapers, the harvesters of earth's abundance. Water and earth being the
elements of the lower world, they dance before the goddesses of the
heavenly worlds of air and fire, symbolising the marriage of heaven
and earth.

The dance is disrupted by Prospero's thoughts interrupting the flow
of his creative imagination, through which all the players in the masque
have become manifest beings. Shakespeare gives the stage direction:

> Prospero starts suddenly, and speaks; after which, to a strange hollow,
> and confused noise, they heavily vanish.
>
> 4.1.138–9

As Prospero's concentration is withdrawn, the impression given is that
of an old gramophone record running down. His imagination dissolves the proceedings and the characters vanish as the remembrance
intervenes of how he should be dealing with the plot against his life by
Caliban and his confederates.

Caliban represents the baser instincts, those connected with the
earth, and it is in these terms that Prospero first addresses him:

> What, ho! Slave! Caliban!
> Thou earth, thou! Speak.
>
> 1.2.315–16

Apart from Ariel, the imprisoned imagination, Caliban was the only inhabitant of the island when Prospero arrived. Prospero's first tasks, were to release Ariel, his imagination, and to bring Caliban, his baser instincts, under control, making servants of them both. Although Caliban performs manual tasks for Prospero, he is still not completely tamed. At first Prospero made much of him and Caliban helped with his material needs, telling him where to find food and water on the island, while Miranda taught Caliban the art of speech. Then he tried to rape Miranda. This was a violation of the soul, for which Calban descended deep into the underworld cave, and it is in a rocky cave that Prospero confines him, letting him loose only to perform his duties. There is no suggestion that Prospero attempted to rape his own daughter, but Caliban's deed represents his master's sexuality, a basic instinct that needs to be controlled. Realising that what is raw and untamed should be treated with severity rather than compassion until it is completely under control, Prospero threatens Caliban with physical pain, side-stitches, cramps and aching limbs, if he doesn't behave himself. This would be in accord with the self-inflicted pain of flagellation and the hair shirt used by those wishing to control their lower natures. It is an example of art cultivating the wildness of nature that Polixenes speaks of in *The Winter's Tale*:[4]

> This is an art
> Which does mend nature—change it rather—but
> The art itself is nature.
>
> 4.4.95–7

In return, Caliban curses Prospero's harsh treatment of him. When he meets the shipwrecked Stephano and Trinculo, Alonso's butler and jester, they introduce him to the delights of alcohol. Caliban begins to worship them as gods for giving him this new experience of drink and, in a drunken orgy, they plan to kill Prospero, believing they can make Stephano king of the island in his stead. While Caliban's responses to sensual stimuli are raw and uncultivated, the butler and jester introduce the influence of so-called civilisation on the basic faculties, with its material desires for riches and power. But Prospero has all this under his observation. Obeying his orders, Ariel leads all three in a painful progress through briers and thorns, eventually dumping them in a filthy pond. He then presents them with a washing line full of rich garments with which they eagerly adorn themselves. They are the very epitome of the outward show being not itself as they strut in their borrowed finery. Stephano, they all believe, can become king of the island if Prospero is removed:

O King Stephano! O peer! O worthy Stephano! look what a wardrobe here is for thee!
4.1.222–3

However Prospero, with the help of his imagination, Ariel, conjures up more spirits in the form of hounds and the drunkards are hunted down like animals. Bacon uses the same imagery when he writes of 'hounding nature in her wanderings, to be able to bring her to the same place again'.[5] Finally, as a last punishment for the rebellious lower nature, further spirits are charged with twisting them into painful convulsions and contortions:

Go charge my goblins that they grind their joints
With dry convulsions; shorten up their sinews
With aged cramps; and more pinch-spotted make them
Than pard or cat o' mountain.
4.1.258–61

This treatment has the effect of bringing them to their senses and they recognise their proper place in the hierarchy of the worlds. Prospero forgives them and, after returning the butler and the jester to their own master, the King of Naples, he accepts Caliban as his own lower nature: 'This thing of darkness I acknowledge mine' (5.1.275–6). Thus acknowledged, Caliban is given a sense of purpose and a recognition of the virtuous life:

I'll be wise hereafter,
And seek for grace. What a thrice-double ass
Was I, to take this drunkard for a god,
And worship this dull fool.
5.1.294–7

The washing line on which Ariel hangs the gaudy clothes for the servants has a symbolic connection with the lime-grove where Ariel keeps the lords in limbo. The linden tree is the same as the lime tree, which is also called a 'line'—in fact the Folio gives 'line grove'—and the servants are caught by the attraction of the brightly coloured garments on a clothes line. This line is nothing other than the lower end of the golden chain that was described in the chapter on *The Comedy of Errors*, stretching from God to the very depths of the creation and linking all the worlds. It also corresponds with Ficino's image of the lover being drawn back to God like a fish at the end of a line. And so, as Ferdinand is drawn to Miranda, both sets of nobles and servants are duly hooked and reeled in to their proper places in the hierarchy of Prospero's worlds.

The play is full of music, as if Prospero is orchestrating his worlds into one glorious symphony; at the same time he uses the bait of music to draw them together. Ferdinand is caught by Ariel's song, the courtiers by the sweet music played at the banquet and even Caliban is aware of the music that beckons him to finer things. The ray of divine light reaches through the prison bars of the material world and, drawn by the harmony, the soul rises towards the music of the celestial spheres. The vision or the dream has more reality than the deeper shadows of the material world:

> the isle is full of noises,
> Sounds and sweet airs, that give delight, and hurt not,
> Sometimes a thousand twangling instruments
> Will hum about mine ears; and sometimes voices,
> That, if I then had wak'd after long sleep,
> Would make me sleep again: and then, in dreaming,
> The clouds methought would open, and show riches
> Ready to drop upon me; that, when I wak'd,
> I cried to dream again.

3.2.133–41

As the play draws to a close, Prospero still needs his 'so potent Art' to produce heavenly music so that his worlds may finally be brought into harmony. When this is accomplished, his staff and books may be buried in the earthly elements to which they belong and for which he has no longer any need:

> But this rough magic
> I here abjure; and, when I have requir'd
> Some heavenly music,—which even now I do,—
> To work mine end upon their senses, that
> This airy charm is for, I'll break my staff,
> Bury it certain fadoms in the earth,
> And deeper than did ever plummet sound
> I'll drown my book.

                              5.1.50–7

He exchanges his magical robes for the attire of the Duke of Milan and, having assumed the outward appearance of god-like man, he prepares for his inner goal. The lords having been drawn into his presence by the heavenly music, Prospero gives these earthly inhabitants a glimpse of the angelic world by revealing Miranda and Ferdinand playing chess in Prospero's cell. Chess is a game of the mind and, within the cell of the magus, the lovers are seated in the heavenly world. Their marriage is, indeed, one of true minds, having reached the constant heart of the angelic world, 'the ever fixed mark, that looks on tempests and is never shaken' (Sonnet 116).

Alonso is overjoyed to be reunited with his son, whom he thought drowned; and Miranda, seeing the reunited passengers and crew of the shipwrecked boat, is amazed at the goodness and beauty of mankind:

> O, wonder!
> How many goodly creatures are there here!
> How beauteous mankind is! O brave new world,
> That has such people in 't!

                              5.1.181–4

Prospero's last words of the play are to bid all those gathered around him, all his worlds, to 'please you, draw near'. Having brought them all together in harmony within himself, Prospero must now let them go. In order to rise above all the worlds to the godhead, he must be free of all attachments. His final act is to release himself from the divine spark of the creative imagination, his last link with the world of manifestation that has also been its creator. And so, when his final task of ensuring a safe passage home for the King of Naples and the lords is completed, Ariel will be free to return to the elements.

All that remains is the epilogue, which Prospero addresses to his audience. He tells them that he is left with no 'spirits to enforce, Art to enchant', but only with the merciful prayers of others, for which he asks the indulgence of the audience. If this is granted, the Duke of Milan may truly be himself, free to return to the divine source of his being:

> Now I want
> Spirits to enforce, Art to enchant;
> And my ending is despair,
> Unless I be reliev'd by prayer,
> Which pierces so, that it assaults
> Mercy itself, and frees all faults,
> As you from crimes would pardon'd be,
> Let your indulgence set me free.

CHAPTER FIFTEEN

How Like a God

------◆·◆·◆------

I N HIS TRANSCENDENCE of all the worlds, Prospero has followed the Platonic path. The Promethean fire of love that, as a
younger man we may believe he saw, like Berowne, sparkling in
a woman's eyes, has risen to enlighten the power of the imagination.
By freeing Ariel he has sacrificed this power so that he may, through
grace, become one with the creative mind of God.

Shakespeare wrote *The Tempest* towards the end of his life and in this,
and his other late plays, he describes the final steps on the path of love.
At this point, it is useful to remind ourselves of where it all began. He
had embarked on the theme of love from the days of his earliest comedies, in which the divine ray often took the form of Cupid's dart. In
the following sonnet, a handmaiden of the chaste goddess of nature,
Diana, steals Cupid's flaming arrow as he lies sleeping and plunges
it into a cold spring. However, it is not entirely extinguished as the
heat of the fiery dart turns the pool into a hot bath with the capacity
to cure all manner of physical ailments. In other words, unblemished
nature, determined to quench the creative ray of love, has plunged the
Promethean fire so deeply into the material world that its spiritual light
has all but faded, although sufficient heat remains in the divine spark
to have some effect, at least on the physical body. Love, however, is
re-kindled at the fire of his mistress' eyes and Cupid's dart wounds
Shakespeare through his heart. Sick with love, the poet turns to the
remedy of the warm bath, but nothing can cure him in the physical
world; the love awakened by the light of heavenly beauty is where his
help lies:

> Cupid laid by his brand and fell asleep.
> A maid of Dian's this advantage found,

And his love-kindling fire did quickly steep
In a cold valley-fountain of that ground,
Which borrowed from this holy fire of love
A dateless lively heat, still to endure,
And grew a seething bath which men yet prove
Against strange maladies a sovereign cure.
But at my mistress' eye love's brand new fired,
The boy for trial needs would touch my breast.
I, sick withal, the help of bath desired,
And thither hied, a sad distempered guest,
But found no cure; the bath for my help lies
Where Cupid got new fire: my mistress' eyes.

Sonnet 153

Shakespeare could not have written so profoundly on love if he had not followed this path himself. There is no doubt that he both loved and understood the nature of man. The endless parade of rounded characters at every level of being, kings and commoners, old and young, are responsible for much of Shakespeare's everlasting and universal appeal. But, above all, he saw them as what they truly are, as universal man, and portrayed them in relation to that image. Cleopatra's vision of Antony is an example of the potential nature of man.[1]

In the macrocosm all men are one, one body, as Menenius calls the citizens of Rome in *Coriolanus*; but, as we have discovered, Shakespeare shows how each character or individual pertains more particularly to one or other of the inner worlds of the complete human being. A description of how one may be led to true knowledge of the nature of man is given by Ficino in *De Amore*. He is writing of the growth of understanding that arises from the first sight of a man's physical form, to what is perceived of that man by the reasonable mind, and finally to how, through the real vision of imagination, the true nature of man is known in the angelic mind. This knowledge may be realised by both the perceived and the perceiver:

When anyone sees a man with his eyes, he creates an image of the man in his imagination and then ponders for a long time, trying to judge that image. Then he raises the eye of his intellect to look up to the Reason of Man which is present in the divine light. Then suddenly from the divine light a spark shines forth to his intellect and the true nature itself of Man is understood.[2]

It is from this same realm of the imagination in the angelic world that, a hundred years later, Shakespeare wrote of his own vision of the true nature of man. Hamlet may have fallen into darkness, but he was still able to speak with the inspiration of the angelic world:

> What a piece of work is a man! How noble in reason! How infinite in faculty! In form and moving how express and admirable! In action, how like an angel! In apprehension, how like a god!

2.2.303–6

Shakespeare believed, with Plato and Ficino, that man could become a god, that in truth he *is* a god, but cannot comprehend it until he has undergone the journey through the worlds. He would then become, as Diotima tells Socrates in *The Symposium,* 'a favourite of the Gods; and at length would be, if any man ever be, himself one of the immortals'.[3] How this would be, as Bottom says of his rare vision, it is 'past the wit of man to say' (*Dream* 4.1.204).

Plotinus wrote of three types of men. Firstly, there are those who live entirely through sensory perceptions and are ruled by the rational mind. Their souls are unable to fly any higher because, having taken so much from the earth, they are weighed down by it. The second type have been urged by the higher part of the soul to fly higher but, unable to see what is above, they have settled for the practical life.[4] The third type, however, are god-like men, exemplified by Shakespeare in Prospero, who is about to return to his own well-ordered country:

> But there is a third kind of god-like men who, by their greater power and the sharpness of their eyes as if by a special keen-sightedness, see the glory above and are raised to it as if above the clouds and the mist of this lower world and remain there, overlooking all things here below and delighting in the true region which is their own, like a man who has come home after long wandering to his own well-ordered country.[5]

Shakespeare not only writes about this ancient teaching but the very words of his plays themselves also have a remarkable effect on all who share them, whether as audience, readers or actors. Those who hear his words never fail to be uplifted and inspired. Coleridge, himself a Platonist and the most perceptive of Shakespeare's critics, wrote that the true poet brings the diffuse parts of the soul into unity through the power of the imagination:

> He. . . brings the whole soul of man into activity, with the subordination of its faculties to each other according to their relative worth and dignity. He diffuses a tone and spirit of unity that blends and, as it were, fuses each into each, by that synthetic and magical power to which I would exclusively appropriate the name of Imagination.[6]

As Prospero, with the help of Ariel, moved the characters on his island according to his imagination, so Shakespeare created his plays in the angelic mind and brought them into manifestation in the earthly world of his theatre, aptly named the Globe. His point of view was from the unity of the whole, looking down, as it were, on all the worlds. In his comedies he drew those worlds into harmony, in the tragedies he revealed the causes of their disruption and, with the help of his muse, the fire of love, he wrote with divine inspiration.

Appendix

From Diotima's Speech to Socrates on the Ascent of Love[1]

WHOEVER THEN ENTERS upon this great affair [the ascent of love] in a proper manner, and begins according to a right method, must have been from his earliest youth conversant with bodies that are beautiful. Prepared by this acquaintance with beauty, he must, in the first place, if his leader lead aright,[2] fall in love with some one particular person, fair and beauteous; and on her beget fine sentiments and fair discourse. He must afterwards consider, that the beauty of outward form, that which he admires so highly in his favourite fair one, is sister to a beauty of the same kind, which he cannot but see in some other fair. If he can then pursue this corporeal beauty, and trace it wherever it is to be found, throughout the human species, he must want understanding not to conceive, that beauty is one and the same thing in all beauteous bodies. With this conception in his mind, he must become a lover of all visible forms, which are partakers of this beauty; and in consequence of this general love, he must moderate the excess of that passion for one only female form, which had hitherto engrossed him wholly: for he cannot now entertain thoughts extravagantly high of the beauty of any particular fair one, a beauty not peculiar to her, but which she partakes of in common with all other corporeal forms that are beauteous. After this, if he thinks rightly, and knows to estimate the value of things justly, he will esteem that beauty which is inward, and lies deep in the soul, to be of greater value and worthy of more regard than that which is outward, and adorns only the body. As soon, therefore, as he meets with a person of a beauteous soul and generous nature, though flowering forth but a little in superficial beauty, with this little he is satisfied; he has all he wants; he truly loves, and assiduously employs all his thoughts and all his care on the object of

164

his affection. Researching in his mind and memory, he draws forth, he generates such notions of things, such reasonings and discourses, as may best improve his beloved in virtue. Thus he arrives, of course, to view beauty in the arts, the subjects of discipline and study; and comes to discover, that beauty is congenial in them all. He now, therefore, accounts all beauty corporeal to be of mean and inconsiderable value, as being but a small and inconsiderable part of beauty. From the arts he proceeds further to the sciences, and beholds beauty no less in these. And by this time having seen, and now considering within himself, that beauty is manifold and various, he is no longer, like one of our domestics who has conceived a particular affection for some child of the family, a mean and illiberal slave to the beauty of any one particular, whether person or art, study or practice; but betaking himself to the ample sea of beauty, and surveying it with the eye of intellect, he begets many beautiful and magnificent reasonings, and dianoëtic conceptions in prolific philosophy, till thus being strengthened and increased, he perceives what that one science is which is so singularly great, as to be the science of so singularly great a beauty. But now try, continued she, to give me all the attention you are master of. Whoever then is advanced thus far in the mysteries of Love by a right and regular progress of contemplation, approaching new to perfect intuition, suddenly he will discover, bursting into view, a beauty astonishingly admirable; that very beauty, to the gaining a sight of which the aim of all his preceding studies and labours had been directed: a beauty, whose peculiar characters are these: In the first place, it never had a beginning, nor will ever have an end, but always IS, and always flourishes in perfection, unsusceptible of growth or of decay. In the next place, it is not beautiful only when looked at one way, or seen in one light; at the same time that, viewed another way, or seen in some other light, it is far from being beautiful: it is not beautiful only at certain times, or with reference only to certain circumstances of things; being at other times, or when things are otherwise circumstanced, quite the contrary: nor is it beautiful only in some places, or as it appears to some persons; whilst in other places, and to other persons, its appearance is the reverse of beautiful. Nor can this beauty, which is indeed no other than the beautiful itself, ever be the object of imagination; as if it had some face or hands of its own, or any other parts belonging to body: nor is it some particular reason nor some particular science. It resides not in any other being, not in any animal, for instance; nor in the earth, nor in the heavens, nor in any other part of the universe: but, simple and separate from other things, it subsists alone with itself, and possesses an essence eternally uniform. All other forms which are beauteous participate of this; but in such a manner they participate, that by their generation or destruction this suffers no diminution, receives no addition, nor undergoes any kind of alteration. When from those lower beauties, reascending by the right way of Love, a man begins to gain a sight of this supreme beauty, he must have almost attained somewhat of his end. Now to go, or to be led by another, along the right way of Love, is this: beginning from those beauties of lower rank, to proceed in a continual ascent, all the way proposing this highest beauty as the end; and using the rest but as so many steps in the ascent; to proceed from one to two, from two to all beauteous bodies; from the beauty of bodies to that of souls; from the beauty of souls to that of arts; from the beauty of arts to that of disciplines; until at length from the disciplines he arrives at that discipline which is the discipline of no other thing than of that supreme beauty; and thus finally attains to know what is the beautiful itself. Here is to be found, dear Socrates, said the stranger-prophetess, here if any where, the happy life, the ultimate object of desire to man: it is to live in beholding this consummate beauty; the sight of which if you ever attain, it will appear not to be in gold, nor in magnificent attire, nor in beautiful youths or damsels: with such, however, at present, many of you are so entirely taken up, and with the sight of them so absolutely charmed, that you would rejoice to spend your whole lives, were it possible, in the presence of those enchanting objects, without any thoughts of eating or drinking, but feasting your eyes only with their beauty, and living always in the bare sight of it. If this be so, what effect, think you, would the sight of beauty itself have upon a man, were he to see it pure and genuine, not corrupted and stained all over with the mixture of flesh, and colours, and much more of like perishing and fading trash; but were able to view that divine essence, the beautiful itself, in its own simplicity of form? Think you, said she, that the life of such a man would be contemptible or mean; of the man who always directed his eye toward the right object, who looked always at real beauty, and was conversant with it continually?

Perceive you not, said she, that in beholding the beautiful with that eye, with which alone it is possible to behold it, thus, and thus only, could a man ever attain to generate, not the images or semblances of virtue, as not having his intimate commerce with an image or a semblance; but virtue true, real, and substantial, from the converse and embraces of that which is real and true. Thus begetting true virtue, and bringing her up till she is grown mature, he would become a favourite of the Gods; and at length would be, if any man ever be, himself one of the immortals.

Notes

PREFACE

1 'Ficino and Shakespeare', in *Friend to Mankind*, ed. Michael Shepherd, Shepheard-Walwyn (Publishers), London, 1999.

CHAPTER 1

1 *The Letters of Marsilio Ficino,* Vol. 1, Shepheard-Walwyn (Publishers), London, 1975, letter 42, p.84.

2 For a full explanation of the Platonic worlds, see Tim Addey, *The Seven Myths of the Soul,* Prometheus Trust, 2000, p.12.

3 Marsilio Ficino, *Commentary on Plato's Symposium on Love,* trans. Sears Jayne, Spring Publications, Dallas, 1985, p.40.

4 'Man' in this context is used in the sense of either gender throughout the book.

5 *Letters* 1.42, p.84.

6 *Ibid.* pp.84-5.

7 *Comm.* p.113.

8 Stephen Orgel and Roy Strong, *Inigo Jones,* University of California, 1973, p.13.

9 *Ibid.* p.1.

CHAPTER 2

1 See Appendix.

2 *Comm.* p.80.

3 Ben Jonson, *Ben Jonson,* ed. Herford and Simpson, Vol. VII, Oxford, 1941, p.193.

4 See note, Arden edn.

5 *Comm.* p.108.

6 This headpiece was used by printers other than those of the Folio for works including the *Psalms,* Spencer's *Faerie Queen* and Bacon's *Novum Organum.* See Peter Dawkins, *Arcadia,* Francis Bacon Research Trust, 1988, pp.226-8.

7 *Letters* 1.110, p.164.

8 *Comm.* p.54.

9 *Comm.* p.172.

10 *Letters* 1.7, p.43.

11 *Ibid.*

12 *Comm.* p.142.

13 *Ibid.* p.46.

14 *Phaedrus,* 252, in *The Dialogues of Plato,* trans. Benjamin Jowett, Oxford, 1892.

CHAPTER 3

1 *Comm.* p.49.

2 *Corpus Hermeticum*, Book 11.7, in *The Way of Hermes*, trans. Salaman, van Oyen and Wharton, Duckworth, London, 1999, p.54.

3 Francis Bacon, 'The Advancement of Learning', in *The Essays of Lord Bacon including his Moral and Historical Works*, Frederick Warne, London, 1883, p.188.

4 Plotinus, 'On the Intelligible Beauty', *Enneads,* Vol. V.8, Loeb's Classical Library, Harvard and London, 1984, p.239.

5 Francis Bacon, 'Wisdom of the Ancients: Pan, or Nature', in *The Essays of Lord Bacon*, p.281.

6 *Ibid.*

7 Apuleius, *The Golden Ass*, trans. Robert Graves, Penguin, 1950, p.271.

8 *The Letters of Marsilio Ficino,* Vol. 4, Shepheard-Walwyn (Publishers), London, 1988, letter 46, pp.62–3.

CHAPTER 4

1 See Chapter 1, p.9.

CHAPTER 5

1 *Jonson* VII, p.221.

2 *The Poems of Sir John Davies,* ed. Robert Krueger, Oxford, 1975, p.115.

3 *Jonson* VII, p.193.

4 *Letters* 1.7, p.44.

5 *Jonson* VII, pp.186–8.

6 *Letters* 1.7, p.45.

7 *Cratylus*, 405, in *The Dialogues of Plato,* trans. Benjamin Jowett, Oxford, 1892.

8 *Letters* 1.7, p.45.

9 *Ibid.* pp.45–6.

CHAPTER 6

1 *Letters* 1.6, p.41.

2 *Ibid.* 7, p.44.

3   *Corpus Hermeticum*, Book 5.1, p.34.

4   *Letters* 1.7, p.46.

5   *Phaedrus* 244–5.

6   Coleridge, S.T. *Biographia Literaria,* ed. J. Shawcross, Oxford, 1979, Vol. I, pp.304–5.

7   Plotinus, 'On Intellect, the Forms and Being', *Enneads*, Vol. V.9, trans. A.H. Armstrong, Loeb Classical Library, Harvard and London, 1984, p.287.

8   *Phaedrus* 244.

CHAPTER 7

1   *Comm.* p.139.

2   Latin, *sub* under, *stare* stand.

3   Bacon, 'Wisdom of the Ancients: Proteus and Matter', p.293.

4   *Comm.* p.48.

CHAPTER 8

1   *Comm.* p.139.

2   *Letters* 1.78, p.124.

3   *Comm.* p.135.

4   *Ibid.* p.139.

5   *Letters* 1.110, p.165.

CHAPTER 9

1   *Letters* 4.46, p.63.

2   *Comm.* p.97.

3   *Ibid.* p.118.

4   *Letters* 1.42. p.85.

5   *Letters* 1.110, p.165.

CHAPTER 10

1   *Corpus Hermeticum,* Book 11.7, p.54.

2   *Comm.* p.111.

3   See Chapter 3, p.40.

4   Bacon, 'The Wisdom of the Ancients: Pan, or Nature', p.280.

CHAPTER 11

1   *Comm.* p.65.

2   *Ibid.* pp.51–2.

3   See Chapter 5, p.48.

4 Macrobius, *Commentary on the Dream of Scipio,* trans. Stahl, Columbia University Press, 1952, pp.100–1.

5 *Letters* 1.13, p.52.

6 *Letters* 1.4, p.38.

CHAPTER 12

1 *Letters* 1.43, pp.85–6.

2 *Select Works of Porphyry,* Thomas Taylor series, Vol. II, Prometheus Trust, 1999, p.148.

3 *Selections from the Notebooks of Leonardo da Vinci,* ed. Irma A. Richter, O.U.P. World's Classics, 1952, pp.262–3.

4 Hermes Tristmegistus, *The Emerald Tablet,* in K. Seligmann, *Magic, Supernaturalism and Religion: A History of Magic,* Grosset and Dunlap, New York, 1968, pp.128–9.

5 See note on *Hamlet* in William Shakespeare, *The Complete Works,* ed. Stanley Wells and Gary Taylor, Oxford, 1986, p.735.

6 *Letters* 1.4, p.45.

CHAPTER 13

1 *Comm.* p.116.

2 *Jonson* p.216.

3 Macrobius, *Commentary on the Dream of Scipio,* p.104.

4 Marsilio Ficino, *Book of Life,* trans. Charles Boer, Spring Publications, Connecticut, 1996, p.127. See also Francis Yates, *Giordano Bruno and the Hermetic Tradition,* Routledge and Kegan Paul, London, 1964, pp.67–9.

5 Bacon, 'Wisdom of the Ancients: Proserpine, or Spirit', p.320.

6 See Chapter 5, p.55.

CHAPTER 14

1 *Letters* 1.6, p.41.

2 See Chapter 10, p.104.

3 Yates, *Bruno,* p.67.

4 See Chapter 3, p.31.

5 Bacon, 'Advancement of Learning', p.176.

CHAPTER 15

1 See Chapter 9, p.96.

2 *Comm.* p.134.

3 See Appendix, p.167.

4 See Chapter 6, p.64.

5 Plotinus, *Enneads,* Book V.9, pp.287–9.

6 *Coleridge on Shakespeare,* ed. Terence Hawkes, Penguin Shakespeare Library, 1969, p.40.

APPENDIX

1 From Plato, *Symposium*, trans. Thomas Taylor and Floyd Sydenham, Prometheus Trust, 2002.

2 'That is, his daemon' (note by Thomas Taylor).

Select Bibliography

Addey, Tim, *The Seven Myths of the Soul,* Prometheus Trust, 2000.

Apuleius, *The Golden Ass,* trans. Robert Graves, Penguin, 1950.

Bacon, Francis, *The Essays of Lord Bacon including his Moral and Historical Works, Advancement of Learning and Wisdom of the Ancients,* Frederick Warne, London, 1883.

Baring, Anne and Cashford, Jules, *The Myth of the Goddess,* Penguin/Arkana, London, 1991.

Cassirer, Kristeller and Randall, ed., *The Renaissance Philosophy of Man*, University of Chicago Press, 1948.

Coleridge, S.T. *Biographia Literaria,* ed. J. Shawcross, Oxford University Press, 1979, Vol. I.

— *Coleridge on Shakespeare,* ed. Terence Hawkes, Penguin Shakespeare Library, London, 1969.

Da Vinci, Leonardo, *Selections from the Notebooks,* ed. Irma A. Richter, O.U.P. World's Classics, 1952.

Davies, John, *Poems,* ed. Robert Krueger, Oxford University Press, 1975.

Dawkins, Peter, *Arcadia,* Francis Bacon Research Trust, Warwicks, 1988.

— The Wisdom of Shakespeare series, I.C. Media Productions, Warwicks, 1998–.

Ficino, Marsilio, *Commentary on Plato's Symposium on Love*, trans. Sears Jayne, second revised edn, Spring Publications, Dallas, 1985.

— *The Letters of Marsilio Ficino*, Vols. 1–7, trans. by the members of the Language Department of the School of Economic Science, Shepheard-Walwyn (Publishers), London, 1975–2003.

— *Platonic Theology,* Vol. 1, trans. Michael J.B. Allen, Harvard University Press, 2001.

— *Book of Life,* trans. Charles Boer, Spring Publications, Connecticut, 1994.

— *Marsilio Ficino: His Theology, His Philosophy, His Legacy,* ed. Michael J.B. Allen and Valery Rees, Brill's Studies in Intellectual History, Leiden, Boston and Köln, 2002.

Godwin, Jocelyn, *The Harmony of the Spheres: A Sourcebook of the Pythagorean Tradition in Music,* Inner Traditions, Vermont, 1993.

— *Music, Mysticism and Magic: A Source Book*, Routledge and Kegan Paul, London, 1986.

Gordon, D.J., 'Hymenaei: Benson's Masque of Union', in *Journal of the Warburg and Courtauld Institutes,* 8, 1945.

Hermes Tristmegistus, *The Way of Hermes*, trans. Clement Salaman, Dorine van Oyen and William D. Wharton, Duckworth, London, 1999.

Hughes, Ted, *Shakespeare and the Goddess of Complete Being*, Faber and Faber, London, 1992.

Jonson, Ben, *Ben Jonson*, ed. C. H. Herford, Percy and Evelyn Simpson, 11 vols., Oxford University Press, 1925–52.

Line, Jill, 'Ficino and Shakespeare', in *Friend to Mankind, Marsilio Ficino,* ed. Michael Shepherd, Shepheard-Walwyn (Publishers), London, 1999.

— 'The Principle of Unity in Shakespeare and Ficino', in *Temenos Academy Review,* London, Spring 2001.

Macrobius, *Dream of Scipio,* trans. William Harris Stahl, Columbia University Press, 1952.

Milne, Joseph, 'Ficino on the Nature of Love and the Beautiful', in *Friend to Mankind, Marsilio Ficino*, ed. Michael Shepherd, Shepheard-Walwyn (Publishers), London, 1999.

Orgel, Stephen and Strong, Roy, *Inigo Jones,* University of California, 1973.

Pico della Mirandola, *A Platonick Discourse upon Love,* ed. Edmund G. Gardner, The Humanist's Library, London, 1914.

Plato, *The Symposium,* trans. Thomas Taylor and Floyer Sydenham, with essays by Plotinus, Guy Wyndham-Jones and Tim Addey, Prometheus Trust, 2002.

— *The Works of Plato*, Vols. 1–5, trans. Thomas Taylor, Prometheus Trust, 1995–6.

— *The Dialogues of Plato,* trans. Benjamin Jowett, Oxford, 1892.

Plotinus, *Enneads*, trans. A.H. Armstrong, Loeb Classical Library, Harvard and London, 1966–88.

Porphyry, *Select Works,* Thomas Taylor series, Vol. II, Prometheus Trust, 1999.

Proclus, *The Theology of Plato,* Thomas Taylor series, Vol. VIII, Prometheus Trust, 1995.

Strohmeier and Westbrook, ed., *Divine Harmony: The Life and Teachings of Pythagoras,* Berkeley Hills Books, California, 1999.

Vyvyan, John, *Shakespeare and the Rose of Love*, Chatto and Windus, London, 1960.

— *Shakespeare and Platonic Beauty,* Chatto and Windus, London, 1961.

Yates, Frances, *Shakespeare's Last Plays*, Routledge and Kegan Paul, London, 1975.

— *Giordano Bruno and the Hermetic Tradition*, Routledge and Kegan Paul, London, 1964.

— *The Rosicrucian Enlightenment*, Routledge and Kegan Paul, London, 1972.

— *The Occult Philosophy,* Routledge and Kegan Paul, London, 1979.

Index